ED & LISA YOUNG

CREATIVE MARRIAGE

THE CREATIVE MARRIAGE

THE ART OF KEEPING YOUR LOVE ALIVE

(EY)

SMALL GROUP STUDIES

Published in Dallas, TX by Creality Publishing.

All Scripture quotations, unless otherwise noted, are taken from The Holy Bible, New
International Version (North American Edition), copyright © 1973, 1978, 1984 by the
International Bible Society. Used by permission of Zondervan Publishing House.

Any emphases or parenthetical comments within Scripture are the author's own.

ISBN 10: 1-934146-00-5
ISBN 13: 978-1-934146-00-2

Cover Design and Layout: Jason Acker
Photos of Ed and Lisa Young: Nicole Nelson

CONTENTS

Small Groups are a vital part of how we do ministry at Fellowship Church just as they are in many churches around the world. There are a number of different theories on how small groups should work and they are all great in different ways. The book you are holding is written with our model in mind. So take a minute to read the following explanation, then feel free to adapt as necessary.

Each of our small groups practices a three part agenda in every meeting. That agenda includes a social time, a discussion time, and a prayer time. Each of these elements share equal importance, but not necessarily equal time. To help you get the most out of this book we have included an explanation of each of the parts.

The first element of every small group meeting should be a time of socializing. This phase of the meeting should be about 30% of your time together. Welcome everyone as they arrive at the host home, make visitors feel welcome by introducing yourself and showing genuine interest in them. Enjoy some snacks, or if your group prefers, a meal together.

Then move on with second part of the meeting, the lesson. The lesson itself may take as much as 50% of your group's meeting time, but remember it is not the most important element. You may want to start this phase of your meeting with a short "icebreaker" to get everyone talking. The questions in the "Start it Up" section of each chapter are what we refer to as "level the playing field" questions that everyone should be able to participate in, regardless of their level of spiritual maturity or Bible knowledge. As your group moves through the "Talk it Up" section in each chapter, remember that it is more important to finish on time than to finish each and every question. It is okay to skip some to be sure you allow enough time to take care of the third phase of the small group time: "Lift it Up."

The "Lift it Up" section is a vital part of every small group meeting and should be about 20% of the meeting. During this time you will be able to share with the group what God is doing in your life as well as asking the group to support you in specific prayers. To help focus this time there are one or two questions at the end of each study that will prompt prayers based on the material you have just talked about. There is also a space for you to write down your prayer request(s) so you don't forget them and so you can communicate them clearly when it is your turn. Below that is a place to write down the prayer requests of the people in your group so you can remember and pray for each request throughout the week.

As an additional tool to assist you in your journey of spiritual development there is a "Step it Up" section at the end of each session. This section consists of five devotional thoughts that reinforce the lesson you've just completed and are designed to help you develop a regular quiet time with God. To get the absolute most from this study I challenge you to take five or ten minutes a day to read and apply these devotionals to your life. If your group meets twice a month or bi-weekly, choose five of the intervening days to incorporate these thoughts into your devotional life.

CREATIVE MARRIAGE

Sometimes people look at my marriage and think, "Wow, Ed and Lisa really have it together. They have been married for over 20 years and are still in love; they have fun together and I'll bet they never fight. Being a pastor must make marriage so easy. If only my marriage could be like that."

Well, Lisa and I do have a great marriage, and I love her more today than ever before. But it is not any easier for us than it is for you. We have worked and continue to work at having a great marriage. Specifically, we work hard at building a creative marriage, because I believe a great marriage is a creative one. God wants you to have a great marriage, too, if you are willing to put in the creative work necessary to make it happen. Having a creative marriage is based on your willingness to do whatever it takes to keep the love, the romance, the intimacy, and the communication in your relationship alive. Notice I did not say it is based on your spouse's willingness to do that. I know how tempting it is, when doing a study like this, to point at your spouse and think things like, "Oh, he so needed to hear that! Get him!, hit him between the eyes," or "She does that to me all the time and she is finally going to hear about it from someone else. I'll just read that part out loud to her."

Don't go there. Too often we become so concerned with what our spouse is or is not doing that we become blind to the fact that we need to make some changes in our own life. So don't focus on your spouse during the coming weeks; focus on yourself. That means no elbows in the ribs during discussions, none of those "ah-hah!" looks, and no finger pointing!

With that in mind, it's time to roll up your sleeves and get ready to do some relational work, as you discover together what it means to have a creative marriage.

CREATIVE FOUNDATION

CREATIVE MARRIAGE

START IT UP

I have said it hundreds of times. At the conclusion of a wedding ceremony I look into the starry eyes of the bride and groom and say, "I now pronounce you husband and wife, in the presence of God and these assembled witnesses." Then I add from the Bible, "What God has joined together, let no man separate."

The man and the woman exchange vows, rings and kisses. And at this point, everything seems so perfect, so right. At that moment, everyone hopes the perfection will last forever. On the day of your wedding, you expect nothing less than relational perfection to last for a lifetime.

Think back to your own big day. For some, that may be just a short jog down memory lane. For others, that special day is tucked behind decades of life. No matter how long ago your wedding was, dust off those memories and answer the following questions.

1. What are some of the most vibrant memories from your wedding day?

_____

_____

_____

_____

2. What were a few of the most prevailing expectations for your marriage on that special day?

_____

_____

_____

_____

On the day of your wedding ceremony, you are convinced that marriage is for keeps. But you add a few kids, a few in-laws, a few financial problems, and the routines of everyday life make a forever marriage seem not so certain anymore.

Some couples tell me, "Ed, we have a great marriage. We are more in love today than we were when we walked down the aisle. Our marriage is great!"

Other couples hopelessly shrug their shoulders and say, "Well, our marriage is about average. It's mediocre. We're just doing time in this prison cell of predictability."

Still others say, "Forever? How about foreclosure? My marriage is hanging by a thread. It's in the deep weeds."

It does not matter if you have a great, average or struggling marriage; there is one powerful reality that you must download. Your marriage matters to God. The marriage relationship is the most important earthly relationship you will ever be a part of. It is the anchor of the family unit. Good marriages can change our communities, our cities, our states, our nation, and even our world. And something this important deserves our undivided attention.

TALK IT UP

You have probably heard someone teach about marriage, or you have read a book, or been a part of a discussion on how to improve your marriage. Chances are, at some point in that study, you heard a statement similar to this, "If you want a healthy marriage, you have to think less about yourself and more about your spouse."

That is common advice for improving your marriage. But during this study I encourage you to do something radically different.

If you want a healthy marriage, during this study you need to think less about your spouse and more about yourself. It might sound unorthodox, but let me explain what I mean.

The tendency for married couples who want to improve their marriage is to put the focus on the other person. Too often, we focus on what our spouse needs to start doing and how we want them to change. But that is not the way to build a strong marriage.

During this series, I'm going to challenge you to ask some I-centered questions:

"What do *I* need to do differently?"
"What should *I* change in order to strengthen my marriage?"
"How should *I* address the issues at hand to help my spouse feel loved and valuable?"

By asking these questions and putting the focus back on yourself and your responsibilities, your marriage has the chance to grow stronger and reach greater heights. Those I-centered questions are actually the key to strengthening your marriage because they expose areas that you can improve by God's grace and with his help.

THE VALUE OF THE VOWS

3. Do you remember the vows you said on your wedding day? Use the blank space below to try to write out your wedding vows. How much do you remember compared to other people in the group?

_____

_____

_____

_____

Your vows are an important part of your marriage. And yet, they are easy to forget. The following is an example of traditional wedding vows:

I, _____, take you, _____, to be my husband/wife, to have and to hold, from this day forward, for better for worse, for richer for poorer, in sickness and in health, to love and to cherish, forsaking all others, until we are separated by death; as God is my witness, I give you this promise.

We make an enormous commitment on our wedding day. In fact, none of us truly knows exactly what we're committing to on our wedding day. We don't realize all of the implications of our words. If we knew all that would be involved in marriage, most of us would probably be too scared to ever get married.

But that's specifically why those marriage vows are so critical. The real value of our vows is something that we can only really understand after years of commitment. Our vows provide a foundation of stability for our marriage. They are a solemn promise that every one of us makes before God, a minister, and our family and friends. When we say those vows, we are promising to remain faithful to the covenant of marriage—no matter what the cost.

A few years ago, I went with Lisa to her twentieth high school reunion. As I walked into the hotel ballroom, the lights were blinking and the dance floor was packed. Videos of the glory days of high school were playing on the side screens, and people twenty years older, with twenty excess pounds, were still trying to "shake that groove thing." It was also twenty times more entertaining to watch than it was in high school!

What was happening at this celebration? The reunion committee was attempting to bring the past into the present. They were trying to make events from twenty years ago current for today.

And that is precisely what you need to do with your vows. Take those promises that you made during your wedding before God and your witnesses and pursue them passionately in the present.

A great way to celebrate your wedding anniversary is to recite your vows to your spouse at least once a year. You don't have to say them word for word the way you did on your wedding day, but put the same sentiment in your own words.

Tell your spouse how much you love him or her. Let your spouse know you are serious about your commitment to love them and that your marriage is not just based on freaky feelings. Remind them of your forever commitment, no matter what happens. Give them an assurance of your love, honor and faithfulness. Let them know that nothing will come between the two of you as long as you live. Bring the promises of the past into the present, pursue them passionately, and continue to move those vows into the future.

I've taken the marriage vows and put them into modern day vernacular that will help you get started:

> *"I commit, before God and you, to creatively*
> *love, honor, and respect you; to be true to*
> *you in all situations—for the rest of my life."*

4. Brainstorm ideas for keeping your vows current in your marriage.

_____

_____

_____

_____

Why are these vows such a big deal? The vows begin, "I commit before God...." We could talk night and day about the value of the vows and how important it is to keep our commitment to our spouse. But it all begins with God.

We have to be on the same page with him and his plans for our marriage. Our understanding and appreciation for the marital commitment flow from the commitment that God (through Christ) has already made to us. When we realize that God loves us unconditionally and took the initiative with us, we will have the endurance and drive necessary for a dynamic and lasting marriage.

> *But God demonstrates his own love for us in this: While we were*
> *still sinners, Christ died for us. Romans 5:8*

5. What does God's willingness to take the initiative in our relationship with him communicate about his commitment to us?

_____

_____

_____

_____

6. How could you apply God's example of love to your marriage?

_____

_____

_____

_____

When you get into a conflict and you feel the temperature rising, remember the value of the vows. When one is in the mood for sex and the other is not, remember the value of the vows. When you get to the end of a tough day, you're in a bad mood and want to lash out at your spouse, remember the value of your vows. When parenting pressures begin to interfere with having a regular date night with your covenant partner, remember the value of the vows. When sickness or financial trouble put a strain on your relationship, remember the value of the vows.

Remember... Remember... Remember.

If I am going to remember the value of the vows—to love, honor, and respect—I have to realize that living out these sacred vows takes roll-up-your-sleeves and grit-under-your-fingernails type work.

A TIRELESS MWE

Recently I boarded a flight and flew out to the west coast. After I took my seat, I noticed a man step on the plane with a look on his face that clearly showed he was having a bad day. He walked through First Class, looked enviously at the empty seats, and sat down in Coach across the aisle from me.

When the flight attendant walked by, this man said, "Excuse me, honey. I noticed some empty seats in First Class. Are there any available?"

She smiled sweetly and replied, "There are some empty seats, but there are none available for you."

The man sat there stewing. After a minute he took out his wallet and thumbed through some cards. The same flight attendant walked back and he said, "Miss, I have this travel agent card and I wondered if you would put me up in First Class now."

She smiled again, said, "No," and kept walking.

What was happening here? This man was trying to get into First Class, but he hadn't paid the price.

The same thing happens in marriage. If you want to have a first class marriage, you have to pay the price. The price tag is hard work; it's something I call the MWE—Marital Work Ethic. And the reward is well worth the payoff.

7. Make a list of the most valuable things in your life. Then discuss the amount of work it takes to attain or maintain each of those valuable things.

_____

_____

_____

_____

We are a society of instant gratification. If it is not quick, easy, express, overnight, or disposable, we don't want anything to do with it. We think, "If it takes a lot of work, there must be another way."

Then, one day, we get married and discover that marriage takes work, negotiation, sweat, toil, pain, and sacrifice—and that it is for keeps. Our disposable culture clashes with the permanency of the marriage relationship. No wonder so many marriages today abandon their vows and end in divorce.

Whatever you do, work at it with all your heart, as working for the Lord, not for men. Colossians 3:23

There are going to be times that you are so angry, so hurt, so crushed by your spouse that you will not want to work on improving your marriage. Those times are specifically when you must remember Colossians 3:23. Even during those times of anger and hurt, God wants you to work with all your heart. He wants you to work at remembering your vows. You not only promised your spouse that you would work on your marriage, you promised God. So when you work in your marriage, you are working for the Lord.

8. When are some of the times it is most difficult to work at improving your marriage?

_____

_____

_____

_____

9. What could you do to remind yourself that your work is not only for your spouse, it is for God?

_____

_____

_____

Ask God to develop a tireless Marital Work Ethic within your heart, because marriage takes work. And to carry out that work in positive and consistent ways through decades of change, it not only takes work; it also takes creativity.

KEEPING IT CREATIVE

Creativity in your relationship is a badge of honor before you get married... the well-planned dates, the unexpected gifts, the love notes and cards and much more.

Then there is the proposal.

Men go out of their way to make special reservations, order the best flowers, search for the perfect ring and much more—all to make that moment just right.

10. What are some of the creative things you did for each other before you were married, or in the early days of your marriage?

_____

_____

_____

_____

It is amazing how quickly creativity can fade in a marriage. The creative work that once brought excitement and passion to the relationship gets replaced with routines and excuses. And we ignore one of the foundational characteristics of God... creativity.

In the beginning God created.... Genesis 1:1

If you have any questions about God's creativity, all you have to do is take a glimpse at creation. From the beauty of the landscape to the variety of animals to the marvels of the human body, there are countless examples of God's creativity throughout the world.

11. Why do you think God's characteristic of creativity gets ignored or moved down the priority list in marriage?

_____

_____

_____

Doing things the same old way just won't work, because our needs are moving targets. And those needs can only be met when you study your spouse. You have to really understand the other person if you want to meet their needs. Love in a marriage flourishes when both partners are working to meet the needs of the other. This doesn't come easily, but it is well worth the effort.

Our marriage has taken a lot of work for Lisa and me, but the work is worth it. What I often find is that couples hit a relational sticking point and don't work on the personal junk that is at the root of their problems. Instead, they simply throw in the towel, abandon their vows, and opt for an easy way out—divorce. And rather than looking for creative solutions to their marital problems, they end up taking the same junk into the next marriage...and the next marriage...and the next marriage.

Situations like this get ridiculous quickly. Don't let that happen to your marriage. Work hard now and keep working for as long as it takes. Make a commitment before God to keep creativity in your marriage for the long haul. Say, "God, this deal is for keeps. I am going to make creativity and innovation permanent features in my marriage."

WRAP IT UP

God is doing great things, and he wants to do even greater things in every marriage. My marriage has room for improvement. Your marriage has room for improvement. So let's develop and live out the value of our vows as we commit to a Marital Work Ethic. Marriage is for keeps. And building it with creativity can change the course of your marriage. So ask God to help you discover how to make your marriage more vibrant, more alive, and more creative than ever!

Prayer Requests:

_____

_____

_____

_____

Notes:

_____

_____

_____

_____

_____

_____

_____

_____

_____

_____

_____

_____

_____

_____

_____

_____

_____

_____

_____

_____

_____

STEP IT UP

Take a step further over the next few days and spend some time reflecting on the following devotional thoughts that reinforce the previous session. Use these as reminders to take what you've learned and apply it to your everyday life.

DAY 1

What comes to mind when you think about the characteristics of God? Some would say, "God is holy. He is completely set apart from us because he is perfect."

Someone else might say, "God is all-powerful. He is able to do anything he chooses to do."

And still others would say, "God is wise. He knows all and understands things we are unable to grasp."

While these are all true characteristics of God that we should admire and imitate, there is one characteristic that we often seem to forgot or ignore.

Read Genesis 1:1-2:3

We have heard so much about God being the Creator that it is easy to ignore the implications of that fact. Take some time to think about what you just read. God took the time to creatively come up with the exact shape and size of this planet. He designed the vast array of scenery and spoke the multitude of the earth's inhabitants into existence. He took the time to give them unique abilities and appearances. And with his hands, God very literally created and formed mankind. In all of this, he displayed his creativity.

God's creativity is one of the most vital characteristics that should be imitated in our marriages. We must choose to exercise this foundational characteristic if we want a healthy relationship, because creativity is the key to growth and strength in our marriage. You may think you are ill-equipped to be creative. But remember, you are created in the image of God, the Creator. In you he placed the ability to be creative. Ask him to help you unleash that creativity in your marriage today.

Are you intentionally creative in your marriage?

If not, what is keeping you from being more creative in your marriage?

Notes:

_____

_____

_____

_____

_____

_____

_____

_____

Prayer Requests:

_____

_____

_____

_____

_____

_____

_____

_____

DAY 2

Read Ephesians 5:1

Do you see yourself as a "dearly loved" child of God? That can be a hard thing to embrace, even when you accept the fact that God forgives you. You are more than just forgiven, more than tolerated, more than liked. You are loved as one of God's children. Because of his love for you, God wants the best for you. He wants you to succeed.

As you attempt to imitate him, you must remember that God loves you and he wants you to succeed in being like him. That truth applies to being creative in your marriage as well. God wants to empower you with creative thoughts and the ability to follow through with those ideas. You can do it because you are a "dearly loved" child of God.

Ask God to give you some creative thoughts. Then, spend five minutes dreaming up creative ideas you can implement in your marriage this week. Don't stop at the first idea that comes to mind. Make a list of your favorite ideas, and put them into practice.

Notes:

_____

_____

_____

_____

_____

_____

_____

Prayer Requests:

_____

_____

_____

_____

_____

_____

_____

_____

_____

_____

_____

DAY 3

Read Colossians 3:23-24

Have you ever wondered about the phrases, "piece of cake" or "cake walk"? Some quick research will show that those phrases came from late nineteenth century promenade contests that typically occurred in African American culture. Essentially, the couple with the best stroll would win a cake. So, you could literally just take a leisurely stroll and win a free cake. Today we use that phrase to say that something is easy.

Well, marriage is not a piece of cake or a cake walk. You cannot just leisurely stroll through your relationship and hope to have a prize-winning marriage. Marriage takes work. There are times you have to roll up your sleeves and really dig in.

God expects this type of wholehearted work. In fact, this type of wholehearted work is for God. When you put elbow grease into your marriage, you are actually working for and glorifying God.

Knowing that you are working for God should make it easier to put the work into your marriage, even when you are not happy with your spouse. You are ultimately working to please God, not your spouse. But, as you work to please God, you will end up pleasing your spouse.

When things in your marriage start to get tough, what can you do to remind yourself that you are ultimately working for God?

Notes:

_____

_____

_____

_____

_____

_____

_____

_____

Prayer Requests:

_____

_____

_____

_____

_____

_____

_____

_____

_____

_____

DAY 4

1 Corinthians 9:24-27

Anything worth winning takes work and dedication. It is not just something that happens by chance. Your marriage is the same way. God wants your marriage to have direction and discipline. Great marriages don't just happen by chance. They take work and discipline.

You would probably love for your spouse to read about the need for direction and discipline, but God wants you to hear it. Each person must make his or her own decision. If you want direction and discipline in your marriage, it starts with you making a decision to run your marriage in such a way as to win the prize.

Think about your marriage's direction. If you keep doing what you are right now, what will your marriage be like in ten years?

If it is not headed where you want it to go, and where God wants it to go, what do you need to do to improve the direction of your marriage?

Notes:

_____

_____

_____

_____

_____

_____

_____

_____

Prayer Requests:

_____

_____

_____

_____

_____

_____

_____

_____

_____

_____

DAY 5

Your spouse was clearly in the wrong. It is absolutely his or her fault. You would take some of the blame if you deserved it, but in this case you don't. This whole fight could be over if your spouse would just own up to what he or she did. Instead, your spouse is acting angry and resisting you. What should you do?

Read Romans 5:8

It is sobering to think that while we were clearly in the wrong, absolutely at fault and resistant to God, he chose to bridge the gap and settle the conflict. God made the sacrifice when it was not his fault. God paid the price when it was not his debt. He took the initiative to show his commitment to us even when we were not committed to him.

To have a successful marriage, we should reflect that commitment and initiative with our spouse. We should take the initiative to reconcile conflicts even when we are right. We should show our commitment to the marriage even when we think we are the only one doing any work. We should attempt to show the love that God showed.

What is an area in your marriage that needs you to take initiative like God took in his relationship with you?

Notes:

_____

_____

_____

_____

_____

_____

_____

_____

_____

Prayer Requests:

_____

_____

_____

_____

_____

_____

_____

_____

_____

_____

_____

CREATIVE COMMUNICATION

CREATIVE MARRIAGE

START IT UP

Think back to when you were dating, when everything—especially communication—was just flowing. It seemed so easy and effortless, didn't it? Do you remember those triple-digit phone bills, the long walks, and the two of you closing down restaurants?

1. Pick three words to describe the communication between you and your spouse before you got married.

_____

_____

_____

One of the most dangerous things in marriage is something that many people can't quite put a finger on. After saying, "I do," something happens. Maybe conversation becomes a little routine, a little predictable, and a little stale. Long, romantic phone conversations become voice mail messages left during lunchtime. Talks of dreams and desires, plans and promises, are suddenly one and two word sound bites.

The problem isn't your marriage. Maybe, just maybe, your communication (your talking and listening skills) isn't quite what it used to be.

TALK IT UP

What separates the great marriages from the not-so great ones? Great marriages are made up of men and women who tenaciously tackle the task of great communication. Great marriages don't just happen. These marriages have dedicated husbands and wives who work at their marriage tirelessly, especially in the area of communication.

It all goes back to the tireless Marital Work Ethic (MWE). The commitment to work creatively at regular, strategic communication must come from both partners.

No area in marriage needs innovative action, creativity, and a tireless marital work ethic more than the area of communication, because that is the one thing that influences every other aspect of marriage. As communication goes, so goes conflict resolution. As communication goes, so goes intimacy and romance. As communication goes, so goes sex. The list is endless.

When it comes to handling communication in your marriage you have two options, both of which are outlined in the Apostle Paul's letter to the Ephesians.

> *Do not let any unwholesome talk come out of your mouths, but only what is helpful for building others up according to their needs, that it may benefit those who listen. Ephesians 4:29*

It starts with, "Do not let any unwholesome talk come out of your mouths...." Our first option is unwholesome talk. But what exactly does that word "unwholesome" mean?

On a hot Texas day one summer, I went fishing with Landra, one of my then five year old twins. We had a wonderful time catching perch at a little pond near our house. Landra, like most children, was emotionally attached to each fish and wanted to keep them all. My general rule is to release the fish I catch, but I told Landra she could keep one to show her mother.

I didn't realize, however, how mischievous Landra could be. While she held one fish in her hand—the one I told her she could keep—she had also hidden another fish in the tackle box behind my back.

We drove home and she showed the fish to everyone. Lisa, as always, was a very proud and affirming mom. We even took a picture of the six-inch fish. After that Kodak® moment, I unloaded the truck and put the tackle box in the garage.

Push the clock forward about ten days and add some triple-degree Texas heat. Lisa looked at me one afternoon and said, "Honey, something smells awful in our garage. I think something died in there."

I walked into the garage and sniffed around. As I neared the source, I thought I had detected the smell of a rotten fish. But there was no way a fish could have found its way into our garage. Right?

My nose led me to the corner where I keep my fishing supplies. The smell was coming from, you guessed it, the tackle box. I opened it up and the stench nearly knocked me over—it was horrific! With newfound freedom, the fumes seeped under the door and crept into the house. Needless to say, Lisa was not happy.

The original meaning for the word "unwholesome" is literally "spoiled fish." Husbands and wives, we can spoil our spouse's spirit with our words.

Have you ever been around a couple who reeked of rotten fish? You can smell the unwholesome talk rolling off their tongues. They tear apart self-esteem, using phrases like, "You never...," "You always...," or "Do you realize how fortunate you are to be married to me?" It is unwholesome talk—spoiled fish—and it stinks up more than just the immediate area. The stench seeps into everyone and everything around.

2. What are examples of "spoiled fish" comments you have made while communicating with your spouse?

_____

_____

_____

_____

3. How do "spoiled fish" comments affect your desire to communicate with your spouse?

_____

_____

_____

_____

"Spoiled fish" is one communication option that we have. But I hope you'll agree that it's not our best option. Fortunately, there is another option. Look again at Ephesians 4:29:

> Do not let any unwholesome talk come out of your mouths, but only what is helpful for building others up according to their needs, that it may benefit those who listen.

We can either spoil our spouse's spirit, or we can opt for the better choice and build up and benefit them through positive communication. I should say to Lisa only what is helpful for building her up; comments like, "I admire you for that," or, "You do that so well," or, "I'm so thankful for all that you do."

Nothing compares to the energy that comes from a positive comment from your spouse. A compliment from a co-worker or a friend is nice, but no one has the power to restore you with words like your spouse.

4. What are some ways your spouse has built you up with encouraging comments?

_____

_____

_____

_____

When I communicate words of love to Lisa, God can use my vocal cords to communicate his love for her, his understanding of her, his encouragement to her, and his compassion for her.

The question that begs to be answered is, "How?" You may have blown it in the past, but you do not have to stay there. It will take work. It is tough. But, it's worth it. The following are some things I have learned that have helped my communication, and will help yours too.

TAKE AN E-BREAK

Have you noticed how technology can both help you and hurt you at the same time? I love technology, but I've found that it is an easy way for Lisa and me to get side-tracked from our relationship. I have found taking technology breaks can be a big boost in communicating. In order for these technology breaks to be effective, they must be intentional and strategic. Don't just wait for eyestrain or carpel tunnel syndrome to set in before taking time off from the distractions of technology.

It all comes down to priorities. You need to set priorities and plan times when you are giving full attention to your spouse. Most of us are so wired in, hooked up and freaked out over technology that we allow the digital world to creep in and steal precious moments from our marital relationship.

Here is what Lisa and I have done in our lives. Several times a week, we take what I call a "phone fast." We don't get up when the phone rings. We don't make a move toward the phone. I discovered something awhile back that has helped in this area: I own all of my phones. The phones don't own me. I am not obliged to answer the phone when I don't want to.

5. What are other ways you could take an "e-Break" with your spouse?

_____

_____

_____

_____

We also spend time talking—just the two of us. I have learned that you have to push a lot of these electronic devices away just to get that time in. Are you too hooked up and wired in to connect with your spouse? Could technology be taking away from your communication?

PLAY IN THE RIGHT ZONE

The next suggestion is something that I call respecting your spouse's time zone. If I am going to build up and benefit my spouse; if I am going to become a great communicator with my spouse, I have to respect her time zone.

Have you noticed that opposites attract? Sometimes a night owl will hook up with a morning person. Here is what usually plays out.

Let's say, for example, that the husband is a "PM person" and the wife an "AM person." Sometimes the husband will try to coerce and even shame his morning spouse into flying into his time zone: "Come to my time zone. That is when I am alert. That is when I am hitting on all cylinders. You'll love it, too. Come over here with me." But that just doesn't work, and it's also not fair to your spouse.

> *Timely advice is as lovely as golden apples in a silver basket.*
> *Proverbs 25:11*

When you play in the right zone by communicating when your spouse is best able to listen, it is as if you are giving your spouse precious jewels. If you make it a habit to communicate in the wrong zone, you can experience some disastrous results.

6. Tell about a time you had poor results from trying to communicate with your spouse in the wrong zone.

_____

_____

_____

_____

OBSERVE SPEED-LIMIT SIGNS

Another way to build and benefit our spouse is to observe speed-limit signs. In our helter-skelter society, we have to find ways that will allow us to slow down and exit Busy Boulevard. Or, for the international traveler, lose the Autobahn mentality.

Some of us need to recognize our own speed limits, step on the brakes, and take the off-ramp to a slower and more meaningful life. No matter how much we want to deny it, we all have limits. We are not machines, and we need to stop acting like we are.

Most of us are over-challenged, over-committed and over-stimulated. We are shopping and soccer-ing and recreating our way into oblivion. We are traveling at such high speeds that we will end up hydroplaning over the most important earthly relationship in the world, our relationship with our spouse.

And while we are driving on Busy Boulevard, the conversation usually goes like this:

"How was your day?"
"Fine."
"What's for dinner?"
"I don't know."
"What time is soccer practice?"
"Six."
"I love you."
"I love you, too."

We get into that fast lane and we push the major things, those heartfelt conversations, and those spiritual dialogues to the shoulder of the road. Then one day, during our annual moments of introspection, we look in the rear view mirror, see wreck after wreck in our marriage, and wonder what happened. We continue to live life on Busy Boulevard and zoom right past what should have mattered most to us.

God has designed us to handle all the pressures of life, if we follow his guidelines.

There is a time for everything, and a season for every activity under heaven. Ecclesiastes 3:1

There is a time for everything we need. The problem comes when we get so busy that we start skipping things we need. It takes hard work and commitment to observe speed-limit signs. The natural pull is to get too busy, but you do not have to give in.

PURSUE RECREATIONAL COMPANIONSHIP

Marital communication has the opportunity to bloom and blossom when, as partners and friends, we discover and participate in a mutually enjoyable activity. I'm not talking about sex here. Sorry to disappoint you, guys. Recreation is another vital ingredient for a dynamic marriage. We have to discover a mutually desirable activity where the husband and wife can just play together.

Some of you might say, "Well, we just don't have anything in common any more. We just never talk."

Have you taken the time and effort to find something to do together on a regular basis where you can have fun together? Have you tried exercising together or taking an art class together? It could be skiing. It could be kickboxing. It could be power walking or jogging.

7. Brainstorm a list of recreational activities couples could do together to help communication?

_____

_____

_____

_____

Conversation flourishes during these casual and recreational times together. In fact, you might learn that you talk more freely and comfortably during these times than when you intentionally sit down and try to force the same kind of meaningful conversation.

Let me also add that watching T.V. or movies together is not the kind of recreational activity I am referring to. Television tends to stifle meaningful conversation rather than foster it. I encourage you to find an activity that forces both of you to get off the couch and engage in meaningful communication.

Don't get me wrong, I enjoy watching television and going to the movies from time to time. Lisa and I will go to the movies for a quick escape from reality. But we know that this isn't a substitute for marital communication.

After heading to the movies, we'll go to Starbucks® and talk about the movie. We've found that the combination of a movie and a conversation over a cup of coffee is a wonderful way to unwind from a busy week and build up our marriage at the same time.

DO THE MATH

We can build and benefit our spouse in another way as well. But I warn you: this one is going to hit close to home.

Remember, husbands and wives, the "216 Principle."

Lisa and I have four children and we love them dearly. We would give our lives for our children; they are gifts from God. Recently, though, I was doing some math and I discovered that we are only going to have each child about 216 months from birth until 18 years of age. After that, they are off to college and on their own.

216 months pales in comparison to a lifetime! I am not married to my children. I am married to Lisa. And my marriage to her is more important than my relationship with my kids. A lot of us have that mixed up and out of focus.

When parents begin to revolve their lives around their children, trouble is just around the bend. Couples who do this neglect their marriage, their communication, their intimacy and romance. And one day, after 216 months, they wake up and say to their spouse, "Who in the world are you?" That's why I know it is so important for Lisa and me to make the time at least twice a month to go out on a date together—just the two of us.

It won't be easy to have a regular date night. Most things this valuable do not come easy. There will be scheduling conflicts. There will be child concerns. There will be a host of other things vying for your date time, but you must not give in.

8. What have you done to overcome the obstacles that come with scheduling a date night?

_____

_____

_____

Sometimes, a difficult part of starting up a date night is thinking of things to do. If you do not go out often, you might forget all the opportunities that are out there to enjoy.

9. Brainstorm two lists of options for date nights. Make one list consisting of inexpensive ideas that stay under $20. Then, make a second list of other options for date nights that will cost more.

_____

_____

_____

_____

People often ask Lisa and me about the secret to our great marriage. Granted, we have as a foundation our mutual connection with Christ. But after that, I believe, one of the key ingredients would be the time we spend together, and specifically the date night. We have to fight for it, but it is worth it.

If we have invested wisely in communication and recreation with our spouse, we will be happy and ready for the empty nest at the end of those 216 months.

THE SWEET SIXTEEN

I worked with a gentleman once by the name of RC Smith. RC was a very encouraging person. One afternoon while we were talking, I asked him how he could explain his great marriage. He said that he and his wife, Charlotte, practiced the Sweet Sixteen every day when he came home. When I asked for elaboration, he said that they would look at each other for sixteen minutes and take turns talking and listening.

This is pretty strong advice. But to do this Sweet Sixteen like RC and his wife, you have to do what we've already mentioned. You have to get away from technology and prioritize your marital relationship above that of your kids. Taking this kind of time together right after work may not be the best time for you. That's okay. Do it in the morning or before you go to bed, whatever works best for you. It could be any time of the day, but just remember to be time zone sensitive.

10. When is the best time for you to have a sweet sixteen?

_____

_____

_____

_____

The sweet sixteen might be tough for the husbands. Guys, let me put it in our vernacular. Most of us watch sports interviews. We see or hear the TV personality thrust a microphone into an athlete's face and ask him a question. Then they ask several follow up questions. In other words, they interview him.

Husbands, do the same with your spouse. Come home and ask her how her day was. Then ask her several follow up questions. Don't just act like you are listening. Dive into her world. Put yourself in her shoes.

My dear brothers, take note of this: Everyone should be quick to listen, slow to speak and slow to become angry. James 1:19

Studies indicate that seven percent of communication is done with words, thirty-eight percent with tone, and fifty-five percent with facial expressions. Whether these statistics are exactly accurate or not, the overall principle is evident. You can give your spouse spoiled perch by your looks: the eye roll, various facial expressions, and obvious body language.

When you are listening, you drive the conversation—the listener does, not the talker. But when it is your turn to talk, don't enter what I refer to as "the moan zone." Too many couples just whine to each other. After a steady diet of that, you can smell the spoiled fish. We need to share the tough things, but don't forget the good stuff.

JUST BECAUSE

Finally, to build and benefit your spouse, give a reason-free gift every once in a while. Or, you could write a reason-free note. You won't believe what this will do.

11. What are some reason-free gifts you would like to receive?

_____

_____

_____

_____

The Bible, without question, is the greatest love note written in human history. First John 4:19 says it best, "We love because he first loved us." Let the love example of your Creator motivate you to demonstrate the same kind of love for your spouse. Write notes, give gifts or do whatever it takes to follow the example set by God to love your spouse.

WRAP IT UP

Great communication is not easy. If it was, everyone would have it. The reality is great communication takes tireless MWE, creativity and persistence. If you are trying to overcome a period of bad communication, do not expect instant results. Communicating is a skill and it is developed. As you develop the skill of communicating, take time to celebrate success—big or small.

When you have those moments of intimate honesty, celebrate in your mind. When you turn off the technology and spend moments in conversation, pat yourself on the back. When you push through the desire to clam up after a fight, realize the success of that moment. By celebrating these moments, you will be encouraged to push on and develop healthy communication in your relationship.

To finish, take a small step in developing communication. Spread out where you and your spouse can be separated from the rest of the group. As a couple, spend five to seven minutes talking about what you learned from this lesson on communication. Develop how you will apply what you learned from this session. Talk about how you can start improving your communication this week.

Prayer Requests:

_____

_____

_____

_____

_____

_____

_____

_____

Notes:

_____

_____

_____

_____

_____

_____

_____

_____

_____

_____

_____

STEP IT UP

Take a step further over the next few days and spend some time reflecting on the following devotional thoughts that reinforce the previous session. Use these as reminders to take what you've learned and apply it to your everyday life.

DAY 1

Read Ephesians 4:29

The second part of this verse, "...but only what is helpful for building others up according to their needs," tells us that we have the ability to build up one another through our words. Not only do we have the ability, but also we have the responsibility.

Gentlemen, compliments and praises from you will build your wife's self-esteem and energize her spirit. Ladies, you can boost your husband's confidence by affirming him and giving him recognition. This is how God wants us to communicate with one another.

Focus on the part of the verse that says, "...according to their needs." That means we have to discern situations and learn how to respond. Being a good communicator, like anything else, takes work. Practice positive communication today by building someone up with sincere words of praise and affirmation. Your spouse would be a great person to start with!

Write down 5 complimentary things about your spouse.

Notes:

_____

_____

_____

_____

_____

_____

_____

_____

_____

Prayer Requests:

_____

_____

_____

_____

_____

_____

_____

_____

_____

_____

_____

DAY 2

Read Ephesians 4:29

This verse ends, "...that it may benefit those who listen." Some translations say, "...that it may give grace to those who listen." In other words, God can use your voice to bless and give grace to the people you talk to.

When you communicate words of love to your spouse, God can use your vocal cords to communicate his love for them, his understanding of them, his compassion for them, and his encouragement to them. But you have to play a part in this.

A mouth that is spewing unwholesome talk is not doing what God wants. He uses your voice for benefiting others. Make sure your communication with your spouse is in line with his plan.

Do you want God to use you to communicate his love for your spouse? Do you need to change the way you communicate so he can? Make it a point to build up your spouse every day according to their needs. When you do these things, then your words will benefit those who listen!

What are areas of need you could build into your spouse with your words?

Notes:

_____

_____

_____

_____

_____

_____

_____

_____

Prayer Requests:

_____

_____

_____

_____

_____

_____

_____

_____

_____

_____

_____

DAY 3

Read Proverbs 25:11

What a vivid word-picture! This verse tells us that our words can be as beautiful as a silver basket full of golden apples. Can you picture that? Can you imagine the value of such a treasure? That's the beauty and value of our words when they are appropriately spoken.

How can you begin to speak appropriately to your spouse? Try communicating at a time of day when both of you are awake and alert. Be responsive to your partner's needs and speak in an uplifting way that builds them up and benefits them.

If you are like me, you have some work to do in this area. Let me assure you, the work is well worth it. How would you like, guys, to be able to give your wife beautiful and expensive jewelry every day? Learn to communicate like this and she will be the recipient of verbal jewelry that is more precious than gold or silver.

When is the best time for you to talk with your spouse?

Are your words fine jewelry for your spouse?

Notes:

_____

_____

_____

_____

_____

_____

_____

_____

Prayer Requests:

_____

_____

_____

_____

_____

_____

_____

_____

_____

_____

_____

DAY 4

Read James 1:19

You have likely heard the old saying before, "God gave you two ears and one mouth so you could listen more and talk less." Our culture has become overrun by rudeness in this area.

Here is a revelation: Listening is not waiting for your turn to talk!

The word "listen" is a verb; it is an action word. That means you can't just absorb what is being said like some kind of sponge. To be a good listener you have to be an active listener, which means using more than your ears.

An active listener makes eye contact, observes voice tone, facial expressions and body language. They respond with appropriate facial expressions and body language while the other person is speaking. Becoming an active listener will make you a better communicator.

Becoming a better listener is not hard to do. But, you will have to make a conscious effort. One reward will be a newfound appreciation for your spouse as you begin to hear and understand them better.

Rate your listening ability on a scale of 1 to 10 (1 being practically deaf and 10 being all ears).

How could you improve your listening ability?

Notes:

_____
_____
_____
_____
_____
_____
_____
_____
_____

Prayer Requests:

_____
_____
_____
_____
_____
_____
_____
_____
_____
_____
_____
_____

DAY 5

Read Colossians 3:13

This aspect of communicating creatively is vastly underrated and underutilized. If you are not regularly asking forgiveness from, and extending it to your spouse, then one of two things is happening. Either you are perfect (which is not likely), or you do not grasp the full power of forgiveness.

Forgiving someone who wrongs us does several things. First, it gives the offended person a healthy release for their anger. Next, it paves the way for a relationship to be renewed. Finally, forgiving someone who has offended you is a way to show them God's grace.

Simply said, forgiveness means freedom for all parties involved. The offended is freed from their anger and the offender is freed from their emotional guilt.

Forgiving is one of the most foreign things we are called to do as followers of Christ. There is nothing in our nature that causes us to lean toward forgiving someone who has wronged us. It is sometimes even harder to forgive someone as close as our spouse. But, by doing so, we are reflecting the true nature of the God who made us and loves us.

How do you typically ask for forgiveness?

What is something you have done that you need to ask your spouse's forgiveness for?

Is there any area in which you need to offer your spouse forgiveness?

Notes:

_____

_____

_____

_____

_____

_____

_____

_____

Prayer Requests:

_____

_____

_____

_____

_____

_____

_____

_____

_____

_____

_____

_____

CREATIVE MARRIAGE

CREATIVE CONFLICT

START IT UP

It seems like some people are just made for conflict. They know exactly what to say, when to say it and even how to say it to argue their case convincingly.

Others just seem to get steam-rolled by every conflict. They go silent as soon as the conflict erupts. If they are able to say anything at all, it is almost always the wrong thing.

1. How do you handle conflict? Read through the following scenarios and discuss how you would handle each one.

- **You are standing in the "10 items or less" line at the grocery store when you notice the person in front of you has at least 15 items.**

- **You notice a car pulling out of a parking space in a crowded parking lot. You put your turn signal on and wait for the car to move. Once the car has pulled out of the space, someone cuts in front of you and takes the parking spot.**

- **You are talking with a group of friends when one of them makes an offensive comment about you. You know the friend did not mean for the comment to be offensive, but it was.**

Whether or not you are good at handling it, conflict is a part of life. Conflict will also be a part of your marriage. Even the best marriages have moments of conflict. Some of those conflicts are minor; others may seem like all out war.

TALK IT UP

Marital conflict is a lot like boxing. Husbands and wives step into the ring, square off, and go toe-to-toe. They throw verbal punches, display fancy footwork to dodge the issues, and demonstrate incredible skills of negotiation. The bottom line is that fights, arguments, spats, and brouhahas are inevitable in the realm of marriage.

2. All couples can recall an argument that started as something small. When you look back at those arguments, they may even cause you to laugh. What are some insignificant things that have caused fights in your marriage?

_____

_____

_____

_____

There will be times when lines are drawn in the sand and sides are taken. But unresolved conflict leads to relational drift. And with tear-filled eyes of anger and hurt, you'll find that the two of you will be hugging your respective corner of a king size mattress that suddenly seems too small.

High emotions may tempt you to put on your gloves and go a few ugly rounds with your spouse in a no-holds-barred fight. You may think that head butting, low blows, and excessive clenching should be the norm. After all, you only care about winning. The cost doesn't matter as long as you win, right? Wrong.

Would a professional boxer entertain the thought of stepping into the ring with millions of dollars at stake and a title on the line without first being trained? Would they enter the ring without a general knowledge of the rules that govern boxing? Of course not.

Yet, countless husbands and wives get married and attempt to deal with conflict without the proper training or working knowledge of the general rules that should govern conflict resolution. They attempt to argue and fight with a no-holds-barred mentality that can cause more destruction and devastation to their marriage. But conflict can actually strengthen a marriage if it's done properly.

The following are some ground rules and guidelines for creative conflict resolution in marriage. But before we dive into these eight guidelines and ground rules, think back to your last fight.

What tactics did you use? How loud did you speak? What nonverbal signals were you giving? What issues were being batted back and forth? Were any low blows, head butts or excessive clenching involved?

As you think about how you reacted, I want you to consider how you might have reacted in light of the following ground rules.

GROUND RULE #1: ASSESS THE DAMAGE PRIOR TO LAUNCH

It is so tempting to launch verbal missiles. We love those zingers, those verbal uppercuts that get our point across quickly, don't we?

And so often in an argument, we fire those verbal missiles, manifested often in name-calling, in an attempt to get the upper hand. We compare our spouse to the dog, the cat, or any other person that comes to mind. Quite simply, we label our spouse or compare them.

Marriage is a process of collecting intimate data. Our spouse shares with us feelings, thoughts, and struggles; and we download them into our spirit. When it comes to verbal missiles, we take this sensitive information that we've downloaded during intimate times and we use it to jam our spouse.

A well-aimed verbal missile can halt future growth and even destroy years of previous gains in a marriage. As satisfying as they might feel at the time, the tough reality is that verbal missiles never serve a good purpose.

I've had the opportunity to talk to thousands of married couples and I have never had one tell me, "Ed, that verbal missile did it. That one-liner finally changed her. When I called her that name... When I told him...."

It does not and will not work that way. So assess the inevitable damage before you launch the verbal missile.

3. Evaluate yourself. In a fight, are you frequently tempted to launch verbal missiles? If so, what could you do to help control that urge?

_____

_____

_____

_____

We can launch a verbal missile out in a matter of seconds, but it may take years to repair the damage. And sadly, while we can repair the damage, it often leaves permanent scars. Consider your words carefully and realize the power they wield in your spouse's life.

GROUND RULE #2: WAVE THE BANNER OF GOOD MANNERS

Have you ever noticed that verbal missiles are usually fairly loud and intrusive? The gut-level explosive reactions that usually accompany a verbal fight serve not to disarm an argument, but to aggravate it.

Several months ago, Lisa and I were in an argument. I was raising my voice a little bit when all of a sudden the phone rang. Instantly, I was transformed from an angry spouse into a caring, compassionate pastor.

"Hello? Oh, everything is great here. How are you doing? Thank you so much for calling. Oh, really? Oh, that is wonderful! Congratulations. When is it due? We will be praying for you. Thank you very much. Good bye."

And then I went right back into the argument with Lisa. I had no problem extending courteous and well-mannered speech to the person on the phone. I should have made an even greater effort to extend courtesy to my wife, but I didn't. I blew it.

A gentle answer turns away wrath, but a harsh word stirs up anger. Proverbs 15:1

4. What are some examples of "gentle answers" you can use in the heat of a conflict with your spouse?

_____

_____

_____

_____

Many people think that to change their marriage they need monstrous, miracle-like events to occur. That is not the case. For good marriages to become great marriages, all it takes are small tweaks, because those small tweaks can lead to higher peaks. Learning to wave the banner of good manners in the heat of an argument is one of those tweaks.

GROUND RULE #3: STICK TO THE POINT AND STAY IN THE PRESENT

It is so easy for a conversation, especially a heated conversation, to drift from subject to subject and completely miss the point. And if we are not careful, it can spiral and tailspin into a crash landing.

The husband walks into the kitchen, tired after a long day at the office. The wife, exhausted from dealing with the kids all day, spins on her heels and asks for help.

But rather than hearing the wife's need for help, he replies emotionally, "You are always asking me to help. I am tired and stressed. Do you realize what kind of pressure I am under at work? You are always nagging me—just like your mother does."

Immediately, the wife goes on defense, "Don't bring my mother into this! How about you? You are so lazy. You sit there on the couch and channel surf all the time."

The tailspin intensifies. "Channel surf all the time? You just totally ignore me. We haven't made love in six weeks!"

"Made love? Who would want to do that with you? All you wear around the house are those same stinky college gym shorts every day. You don't comb your hair on the weekend and you always have coffee breath!"

Prepare for a crash landing, we're going down: "Oh Yeah! Well, most women would give their right arm to be married to me and have the things I give you. I am not going to take this anymore. I'm outta here!"

The door slams and a marriage begins to disintegrate.

How did this happen? It all started with a request for help. The wife asked the husband for some help, and from there it spiraled into a tailspin of miscommunication. The in-laws were dragged in, threats were made, sexual frustration and even divorce was mentioned.

This kind of escalation should never occur. We must stick to the issue in order for the conflict to be productive. If the issue is finances, have solution-driven arguments about finances. If the issue is sex, have solution-driven arguments about sex. Don't mix the issues when you are experiencing marital conflict. Look for solutions, not sucker-punches. Also, stay in the present tense. Don't bring up old arguments that should have been settled long ago.

5. Why do you think it is tempting to drag up the past or other issues in arguments?

_____

_____

_____

_____

6. What could you do to help put a conflict behind you when it is over?

_____

_____

_____

_____

For I will forgive their wickedness and will remember their sins no more. Hebrews 8:12

For if you forgive men when they sin against you, your heavenly Father will also forgive you. But if you do not forgive men their sins, your Father will not forgive your sins. Matthew 6:14-15

God is willing to let your past be forgotten and forgive you from your wrongdoing. That should motivate us to forgive our spouse and not drag up the past. It might not be an easy thing to do. But remember how God continually does it for you and emulate that in your marriage.

GROUND RULE #4: AVOID THE SUBTERRANEAN LEVEL

Too many of us are subterranean fighters. Issues of all sizes and importance arise from time to time, but many of us just bury them. Instead of dealing with them when they first surface, we go subterranean with them. We dig a relational hole and bury the problem, hoping it will just go away.

Deep inside, though, all of these unresolved issues are eating away at us. And as we continue to go subterranean with issues, the toxic waste begins to leak into every avenue and aspect of our life.

Don't bury the issues. Deal with them rapidly. Deal with issues when you both are rested and can talk about them. And deal with them, the Bible says, before the sun goes down.

Do not let the sun go down while you are still angry. Ephesians 4:26

I encourage couples to pray together before they go to bed. You'll find it is very difficult to pray together if you are in an argument or in conflict. Many times Lisa and I have had to stay up almost all night resolving issues, because we don't say good night until we have ended the fight. This is a great tactic because it helps us deal with the toxic waste immediately before it has a chance to cause any more damage.

GROUND RULE #5: NEVER USE PSYCHOBABBLE

We have read a few books, taken a few courses, or listened to Dr. Phil and Oprah; so, naturally, we think we can psychoanalyze our spouse. "Oh, you are being so obsessive-compulsive. You are such an enabler. That is classic textbook stuff." But consider what the Bible says about pointing out the flaws in others, especially our spouse.

> Why do you look at the speck of sawdust in your brother's eye and pay no attention to the plank in your own eye? How can you say to your brother, "Let me take the speck out of your eye," when all the time there is a plank in your own eye? You hypocrite, first take the plank out of your own eye, and then you will see clearly to remove the speck from your brother's eye. Matthew 7:3-5

Jesus was using hyperbole here, a little Hebrew humor. Just picture a husband with a Sequoia tree hanging out of his eye while he points out a speck of dust on his wife's contact lens. It sounds ridiculous when you think about. But if you are not careful, you can end up spitting criticism at your spouse while you have a Sequoia tree sticking out from your own eye. When the heat of conflict begins to rise, it's a temptation that we all face.

7. How can you fight the temptation to focus on your spouse's speck while ignoring your own Sequoia tree?

_____

_____

_____

_____

GROUND RULE #6: LISTEN UP WITHOUT WINDING UP

When an argument occurs, a lot of us spend more time getting ready to pounce rather than listening to what our spouse is actually saying. We do a major league windup and cannot wait to throw the fastball at their head, oftentimes while they are still talking. But readiness to pounce and interrupt is a sure sign that we are not really listening.

When we listen, we should make a mental list of what our spouse is saying. Listen for the issue at hand. Then, when they are done, we should repeat back what we heard. That gives our spouse the chance to indicate thumbs up, "Yes, you got what I said," or thumbs down, "No, you misunderstood."

> *He who answers before listening—that is his folly and his shame.*
> *Proverbs 18:13*

Conversation, including heated conversation, is a two-way street. You may think you are having a meaningful conversation with your spouse just because you are articulating your concerns to them. But if you are failing to listen to their concerns, then you are not really conversing with them. All you're doing is lecturing them.

8. What steps have you taken to help you listen more attentively to your spouse?

_____

_____

_____

_____

GROUND RULE #7: MAKE A YOU-TURN

In marriage, we need to make a unique U-turn: a You-Turn. So often in the heat of an argument, we use the word "you" too much. "You always waste money." "You never talk to me."

Instead, we should make a point to use "I feel" statements. "I feel that we should save more money." "I feel like we are not really communicating."

Using "I feel" statements in the place of "You" statements changes the dynamic and direction of the conversation, because revealing your feelings is the beginning of real healing in a relationship.

9. Think about the following issues. Then tell what a "you" statement might be and what a statement after a "you turn" might sound like?

- **Your spouse is spending too much money**

- **Your spouse is not helping you do work around the house**

- **The amount of intimacy in your relationship is lacking**

> *Carry each other's burdens, and in this way you will fulfill the law of Christ. Galatians 6:2*

This is not optional. When you train with weights, you train with another person so they can spot for you. That person is literally sharing the burden.

Similarly, you are to become a relational spotter for your spouse.

If your spouse had a difficult day at work, try asking, "Do you want to talk about it?" Maybe your spouse is feeling down about something their father said to them. Bear their burden by asking, "How can I help?"

It's about sharing and bearing the feelings of another. It removes the "I" factor and reintroduces the "we" factor.

GROUND RULE #8: AVOID THE D-WORD

The ultimate trump card in conflict is the "D-word." Whenever a husband or wife feels really beaten down, this word will get thrown into the mix and usually ends up lighting a powder keg explosion.

Instead of working through the issues or asking for forgiveness, the word divorce is tossed out like a bomb.

"I'm so sick of you. If you talk to me like this one more time, I'm going to divorce you!"

While that is the fastest way to end an argument (though not very beneficial), it is also the fastest way to head for an actual divorce.

10. Why do you think using the D-word can be dangerous in a marriage?

_____

_____

_____

Marriage is all about trust. It is impossible to build trust when one or both of you is threatening to dissolve a covenant that you made with each other before God.

Let me urge you to never use the D-word as a last resort. Instead, work hard to seek creative solutions to your conflict. Remember, God is your biggest source of help and your biggest cheerleader when you find yourself in conflict. Ask him for strength and help to work through your issues in a way that honors him.

11. Describe how God has helped you work through conflict issues in the past.

_____

_____

_____

_____

I could go on and on about these conflict resolution principles. You may have even found some others. But the bottom line is that these principles are all found in the Bible, and they revolve around a commitment by both the husband and wife to deal seriously, radically and rapidly with conflict as it occurs.

WRAP IT UP

Marriage conflict can seem daunting, but there is a cosmic conflict that is the key to all other conflict resolution. I'm talking about a conflict with God. Conflict resolution starts with a step of faith by saying, "Christ, I accept what you did for me and apply it to my life."

Your life and your marriage will never work the way God intended if you have not made that decision and taken that step. But the moment that we receive

Christ and what he did for us on the cross, an awesome thing happens.

> *Therefore, if anyone is in Christ he is a new creation; the old has gone, the new has come! All this is from God, who reconciled us to Himself through Christ and gave us the ministry of reconciliation. 2 Corinthians 5:17-18*

In short, our conflict with God is resolved because Jesus has taken care of the sin problem on our behalf. He modeled for us the ministry of reconciliation. And Christ's gift to us is the key to conflict resolution in our relationships with one another, especially in marriage.

When Christ comes into our lives, he places the person of the Holy Spirit inside of our hearts and the Holy Spirit gives us the extra RPMs to take action in marriage. The Holy Spirit will whisper, "Hey, quit being so selfish. You have been reconciled to God through Christ, something you don't deserve. Now get on the same page and reconcile with your spouse."

If you say that you are ready to get serious with God, you can be a great facilitator in creative conflict resolution. You can do it as you rely on the Spirit of God. But it is a choice that each person has to make. Next week we will be looking at intimacy, because I am confident that conflict resolution done in a biblical way opens the door to greater levels of intimacy.

Prayer Requests:

_____

_____

_____

_____

_____

_____

Notes:

_____

_____

_____

_____

_____

_____

_____

_____

_____

_____

_____

_____

_____

_____

_____

_____

_____

_____

_____

_____

_____

_____

_____

_____

_____

_____

STEP IT UP

Take a step further over the next few days and spend some time reflecting on the following devotional thoughts that reinforce the previous session. Use these as reminders to take what you've learned and apply it to your everyday life.

DAY 1

Read James 3:5-6

Is the conflict in your marriage painful or purposeful? For most of us, marital conflict is just painful. Usually, this is because we fail to be purposeful in our conflict and we miss the positive potential that conflict has.

One way that we destroy the positive potential of conflict is by the harmful words that we hurl at our spouse in the heat of battle. And we use those words like verbal missiles to ignite a scorching fire. And as a result, we end up with a painfully burned spouse and a wasted opportunity for growth in our marriage.

Ask God to show you how your words have been damaging to your spouse in the past. Then ask him to help you approach conflict in the future in ways that will extinguish the flames and lead to positive growth for your marriage.

Notes:

_____

_____

_____

_____

_____

_____

_____

_____

_____

Prayer Requests:

_____

_____

_____

_____

_____

_____

_____

_____

_____

_____

_____

_____

DAY 2

Read James 1:2-4

The best way to achieve muscle growth is by resistance. To know if a steel bar is strong enough to support your weight, you have to try to bend it. When engineers are testing the strength of concrete, they do something called a stress test.

In the same way, marriage is proven strong through resistance, bending, and stress tests. And the greatest way this is accomplished in marriage is through conflict.

Through testing you can gain the trust of your spouse. Each time your spouse sees that you handle conflict in a positive way, they trust you more. As trust grows, your spouse will begin to feel safe enough to open up even more. This is the way that a marriage can mature and grow to the point you can say that it is complete, lacking in nothing.

Did you ever stop to realize that conflict holds this kind of potential? Ask God to give you a new perspective on conflict and show you how you can strengthen your marriage through conflict.

Notes:

_____

_____

_____

_____

_____

_____

_____

_____

_____

Prayer Requests:

_____

_____

_____

_____

_____

_____

_____

_____

_____

_____

_____

DAY 3

Read Luke 6:42

When you enter into conflict, are you the type who only looks at what your spouse did wrong? When it comes to your own wrongdoing, are you more interested in defending it or confessing it?

The Bible is very clear about telling us not to worry about someone else's problem until we have taken a thorough look in the mirror.

It doesn't matter who started the argument in marriage, it is your responsibility to reconcile and come to peace. Many times our feelings have been hurt in some way so we sit, waiting for them to come crawling to us and do their duty.

Instead of falling into that mindset, ask God to help you see the log in your own eye before trying to remove the speck in your spouse's eye. And ask him to give you the courage to be purposeful in coming to a peaceful resolution.

Notes:

_____

_____

_____

_____

_____

_____

_____

_____

Prayer Requests:

_____

_____

_____

_____

_____

_____

_____

_____

_____

_____

_____

DAY 4

Read Ephesians 4:15

Why is it that when we are angry we feel temporarily satisfied by throwing verbal daggers? Have you ever noticed that after the verbal daggers, you feel terrible about what you said in the heat of an argument?

It's okay to directly confront the issues in a conflict. In fact, it's healthy to deal with problems immediately. However, we need to weigh our words and consider if they will be helpful or if they will just be adding fuel to the fire.

Speaking the truth without love can be harsh and hurtful. Speaking love without truth is nothing more than manipulation and fluff. Truth and love must come together so we can reach a resolution.

This is important in both speaking and in listening. In other words, are you willing to speak the truth in love to your spouse? Sometimes it takes a lot of courage to be truthful and sometimes it takes a lot of restraint to love.

How about when you are listening? Are you willing to hear the truth, or are you only willing to listen when someone is making you feel good?

How could you speak the truth in love in the following scenarios?

- *Your spouse planned something special for you, but you do not like what he or she planned.*

- *You planned something special for your spouse, but they did not show you any appreciation.*

Notes:

_____

_____

_____

_____

_____

_____

_____

_____

Prayer Requests:

_____

_____

_____

_____

_____

_____

_____

_____

_____

_____

_____

DAY 5

Read Philippians 2:3-4

Winning an argument is not the goal. Coming to a resolution in conflict is the goal. How different would it be if we would consider our spouse to be more important than ourselves?

Humility means that we want to understand our spouse's needs when we enter into conflict. In other words, we need to be others-focused instead of self-focused.

This is especially important when it's our turn to listen. Don't just talk, and talk, and talk. When you cut off your spouse in mid-sentence to make a point, you aren't considering your spouse better than yourself. You're simply saying, "What you have to say is not important!"

Listening is the most important key to communication. If you are really concerned about our spouse and their needs, then listen to what they have to say. Listen for why they are upset and how they've been hurt.

Think about a few of your recent conflicts. Did you try to win the conflict at all costs? Or did you seek an answer that was beneficial for both of you?

Notes:

_____

_____

_____

_____

_____

_____

_____

_____

Prayer Requests:

_____

_____

_____

_____

_____

_____

_____

_____

_____

_____

_____

CREATIVE MARRIAGE

CREATIVE INTIMACY

START IT UP

When you hear the word "sex," what comes to mind? The mere mention of that word can bring a flood of thoughts and emotions. But I doubt that when you hear it you think about God or any biblical connotations.

There are many voices that speak out when it comes to sex. There is the voice of the sex education teacher saying one thing. There are the messages in songs that range from discreet to blatant. And most television shows and movies communicate something about sex.

1. Explain what voices you think are the most influential when it comes to sex.

_____

_____

_____

_____

In the sexual discussion, God is often viewed as the cosmic killjoy. But that only comes from a misunderstanding of what God says about sex and what he wants us to experience in a sexual relationship.

Of all the voices that speak out on sex, God's is the one voice we should actually listen to. After all, God invented sex. He designed it for our pleasure to use within marriage. God uniquely fashioned us as a male or a female and pre-wired us for sexual desire. So God's Word should be our primary voice in this area, not a drowned out voice covered up by culture.

Sex is a positive thing, a good thing. It is from God and he wants us to experience great sex. He wants to build a great sex life in every marriage. However, research shows that at least a third to one-half of married couples are experiencing a moderate to major level of sexual frustration in marriage. Most marriages are experiencing some major sex busters.

Sex busters are attitudes or habits that keep us from using this God-given gift in a God-ordained way. But connected to each sex buster is a positive flip side, a sex builder. Sex builders help you become the kind of mate, sexually speaking, that God wants you to be. If you want to make love regularly and creatively, you have to understand these sex busters and builders.

TALK IT UP

Whenever I talk about sex in church, I am amazed at how closely people pay attention. No one sleeps. No one drifts off. No one counts ceiling tiles. Some people might think that we shouldn't talk about sex in the church. But those people don't understand what God says about sex in the Bible.

God was not too ashamed to create sex, so we should not be ashamed to talk about sex. In fact, the two most prominent places where we should discuss sex are in the home and at church.

Historically, the church has done a pathetic job in talking about sex. Thankfully, some churches are trying to change that by getting real and talking about what God's Word says about this important subject. And this study is going to help open the topic up in your own marriage and home.

SEX BUSTER #1:
YOU DON'T KNOW WHAT GOD SAYS ABOUT SEX

When couples are unaware of God's take on the subject, unaware of what the Bible says, it becomes a sex buster. The evil one does not want you to have the biblical knowledge, information and application principles regarding sex. He doesn't want you to have a great sex life because, if you do, the bond you have with your spouse will be stronger than super glue. In addition to strengthening the bond, your close sexual relationship with your spouse will provide a firm foundation for great child rearing principles.

2. Do you think most people outside the church believe God is pro-sex? Explain your answer.

_____

_____

_____

_____

3. Why do you think the church has historically avoided teaching about sex in a positive way?

_____

_____

_____

_____

SEX BUILDER #1:
GET IN SYNC WITH SCRIPTURE

When you don't know or understand what God says about something, search for the answer. We have to get in sync with scriptural sexuality. I have talked to numerous couples who have Christ-centered marriages, and they have wonderfully, mutually satisfying sexual relationships. Study after study shows that the most sexually satisfied people in marriage are those who pray together, those who read the Bible together and those who go to church together. They are doing sex the way God wants them to, and their relationship is stronger because of that.

> _The husband should fulfill his marital duty to his wife, and likewise the wife to her husband. The wife's body does not_

belong to her alone but also to her husband. In the same way, the husband's body does not belong to him alone but also to his wife. 1 Corinthians 7:3-4

This verse in 1 Corinthians talks about management. Your spouse is the manager over your body. Look at the passage one more time. Are you in sync with Scripture?

4. How does this biblical principle about sex differ from the common beliefs and teaching of culture today?

_____

_____

_____

_____

SEX BUSTER #2:
YOU DON'T UNDERSTAND YOUR SPOUSE'S SEX DRIVE

We all know men and women are different. We have different physical traits, different perspectives on life, and different takes on parenting.

Sex is no different. And most couples are clueless about how to deal with the sex drive of their spouse. God has wired us differently with unique sex drives. So to help understand your spouse's sex drive, let's take a look at both sides.

A man's sex drive is like an Olympic sprint. In an instant, he is ready to sprint into sex. There's no warm up time needed. A husband experiences sex and then, from his sexual experiences, flow his feelings.

The wife is the polar opposite. A woman's sex drive is more like a 5K run. She more or less jogs into sex. She has to experience the feelings of intimacy before she can experience physical intimacy.

This is where problems develop. The husband, the sprinter, approaches his wife the way he wants to be approached. He is aggressive and initiative taking, and he tries to sprint into sex.

The wife, though, approaches her husband the way she wants to be approached—with romance, intimacy, and gentleness. She expects to jog into sex.

Now you've got some tension and sexual frustration on both sides.

SEX BUILDER #2:
DIAL INTO YOUR SPOUSE'S SEX DRIVE

To experience great sex in your marriage, you must understand what your spouse is feeling and expecting when it comes to sex.

For the most part, men desire sex more than their wives do. This is not the case across the board, but it's true in most situations and circumstances.

Dr. Willard Harley, a Christian psychologist, has a beautiful illustration that really hammers home an understanding of a man's sex drive. Imagine a stool with a glass of water sitting on it. The husband is next to the stool and the wife is next to him, away from the water. The wife is immobilized. She can't get to the water. The husband is the only one who can get the water.

The wife turns to her husband, "Honey, would you please pour me a glass of water? I am getting a little thirsty."

The husband turns and responds, "I don't really feel like it. I am not in the mood. Maybe in a couple of hours."

A few hours roll by and one more time the wife turns to her husband, "Honey, I am getting thirsty. Would you please give me a glass of water?"

The husband responds, "You know, I am tired. I've had a long day, okay?"

Then the wife begins to get angry. She can feel her temperature rising. She wants a glass of water badly at this point, so she begins to demand a drink of water. "Give me a glass of water! You are the only one who can give me the glass of water."

The husband looks at his wife, spins on his heels and says, "You are not going to get any water with an attitude like that!"

The husband returns to the scene about a day later and now the wife is livid. Finally, the husband says, "Fine! Here is your water. Just drink it!"

When the wife is gulping down the water, do you think she is satisfied? Do you think her thirst is really quenched? No. She knows she is going to be thirsty again soon and, if she wants another drink of water, she had better watch what she says to her husband.

So goes a man's sex drive. Like water quenches a physical thirst, sex in marriage quenches his thirst in a physical, spiritual, emotional and psychological manner. For sex to be truly satisfying, it must be given and received in the right spirit of love and compassion.

Now let's pick on the men. Men are so compartmentalized and structured that most of us are clueless when it comes to sex in the overall context of the marital relationship. We are, for the most part, one-dimensional people.

A while back I saw a woman reading a book entitled *All About Men*. As I walked by I looked at her and said, "All about men, huh?"

She said, "Yeah, it's a short book."

Wives, unlike their husbands, are multifaceted and multidimensional. The context surrounding sex is immensely important for them. They have to know that everything is A-okay outside the bedroom before everything gets A-okay in the bedroom.

5. Brainstorm a list of words that you think describe the opposite gender's sex drive.

_____

_____

_____

_____

Yes, there are those times when the husband and wife are both in the mood, when they both want to make love. But what do you do when one is ready for it and the other is not? You get in sync with Sex Builder #2 and dial into your spouse's sex drive.

Husbands, slow down. Quit being a sprinter all the time and jog a little bit with your wife. Sometimes it's fun to jog. And wives, don't always run so slowly. Try incorporating some sprints into that 5K.

Because when the husband is thinking about his wife's needs and the wife is thinking about her husband's needs, you have two people who understand the pace of passion.

SEX BUSTER #3:
YOU HAVE UNREALISTIC IDEAS OF SEX

Because of unrealistic portrayals of sex in music, novels, TV, movies, and other media, many couples have unrealistic expectations when it comes to real life sex. Don't measure your sexual satisfaction through the grid of movies, videos and the secular media. That is not the real story.

6. How have you commonly seen sex portrayed through popular media?

_____

_____

_____

_____

Let me also say something about pornography here. It has become somewhat vogue these days to bring adult videos into the bedroom. Husbands and wives rationalize this by saying that it will give them a boost in the bedroom. That is simply not the case.

First of all, when you bring an adult video into the bedroom, you are involved in lusting after and being aroused by another person or persons. Christ said that if you lust after someone in your heart, you are committing adultery.

Secondly, pornography will always keep you wanting more and more. You will get addicted to the extra stimulation and will start to need it just to be aroused by your spouse.

Pornography has the potential to leave great marriages in an ash heap. And if it is not dealt with seriously and swiftly, it will destroy the intimacy you have with your spouse. So do whatever it takes, now, to remove this incendiary influence from your life—before it's too late.

SEX BUILDER #3:
SEE THROUGH THE SECULAR SMOKE SCREEN

See through the secular smoke screen that distorts the realities of a biblical commitment in marriage. Run your love life through the scriptural grid and see what the Bible says about one man and one woman committed to God and to each other in the context of marriage. Sex should be reserved for a man and woman who are selflessly serving one another with energy and creativity—in marriage. These couples see sex as an opportunity for greater intimacy and mutual discipleship. In short, it's a win-win for these couples.

After speaking on this subject in one of our weekend worship services at Fellowship Church, one lady commented enthusiastically to my wife, Lisa, "I really enjoyed today's message. My husband and I are going to go home and do some discipleship!"

SEX BUSTER #4:
YOU ARE TRASHING THE TEMPLE

This sex buster is one of my favorites, because it such an obvious issue and yet something we often overlook. Pay attention to your grooming and hygiene issues.

Many men, after they get married, say, "Now I can lose the look and gain the weight. I can go on a hygiene hiatus, man." And they forgo the membership at the local gym to become part of the Laz-Y-Boy® brigade.

The wives, on the other hand, end up wearing one of those "Not tonight, honey" nightgowns to bed. I'm talking about the kind that screams "I've got a headache!"

After we say, "I do," we often follow it up with, "I don't." We say, "I don't need to work hard to look good for my spouse anymore." "I don't need to worry about competing for her or dating her." "I don't have to impress him any longer by taking care of my body." But that mentality is a fast track to losing out on the great sexual relationship that God wants you to have with your spouse.

SEX BUILDER #4:
TAKE CARE OF THE TEMPLE

Do you not know that your body is a temple of the Holy Spirit, who is in you, whom you have received from God? You are not your own.... 1 Corinthians 6:19

We have a saying in Texas, "Don't mess with Texas." Well, God is saying, "Don't mess with the temple."

Taking care of your body doesn't equate to turning into a Ken and Barbie® couple or engaging in a physical obsession that can take over your life. It does mean, though, that we need to do the best with what we have.

Eating properly, working out, and staying as lean as possible are acts of worship to God. Romans 12:1 says to, "present your bodies as living sacrifices, holy and pleasing to God." When we take care of our body, our temple, we are expressing love to God and love for our spouse.

I spotted a sign on a taxi one day that read, "It's all about work."

That should be your marital bumper sticker. Remember the MWE, the Marital Work Ethic. It takes hard work to continue courting your spouse by maintaining your physical appearance. Don't neglect the obvious: you can't keep your sex life in shape if you don't keep your body in shape.

7. What could you start this week to take better care of your temple?

_____

_____

_____

_____

SEX BUSTER #5:
YOU ARE MAKING EXCUSES INSTEAD OF MAKING LOVE

When you have a negative response to your spouse's sexual advances, a few things can happen. First of all, you can shame your spouse. By constantly turning your spouse down, you are communicating that something must be wrong with his or her desires or that his or her needs are not legitimate. It takes a certain amount of vulnerability to ask for your sexual needs to be met, and it is embarrassing and defeating for that vulnerability to be rejected.

Secondly, by rejecting your spouse, you can damage your fellowship with God. The marriage relationship is a reflection of the relationship that Christ has with the Church. Because of this unique correlation, when your marriage relationship is strained, your relationship with Christ is also negatively impacted.

Thirdly, you are inviting heightened temptations for both you and your spouse. Sadly, when husbands and wives do not get what they need at home, they will go looking elsewhere for it. The potentially devastating results of the wandering eye are obvious.

8. What are some of the most common excuses for a married couple not having sex, and what percentage of those excuses do you think are legitimate?

_____

_____

_____

_____

SEX BUILDER #5:
STOP DEPRIVING ONE ANOTHER

> *Do not deprive each other except by mutual consent and for a time, so that you may devote yourselves to prayer.*
> *1 Corinthians 7:5*

Aside from certain medical problems or health issues, the only excuse we should give to turn down sex with our spouse is, "I'm in prayer." But you must both be in agreement.

While studying this issue, I spoke with a good friend of mine and he said, "Ed, if the husband and wife do agree to abstain for a time of prayer, I know what the husband will be praying for: Sex!"

I don't think the Bible is telling us that we can never say no. But no should be the exception. And don't just say no. If you say no, say no with an appointment. "No, in a couple of hours," "No, tomorrow morning," or, "No, tomorrow night." This appointment gives the two of you something to look forward to.

At this point, if you are a woman, you may be thinking, "I don't like this study at all. This guy is totally out-of-touch with reality! He is a man and, of course, he is going to say these things."

Well, my wife Lisa co-wrote this material with me, and she didn't think I was being hard enough on the women.

SEX BUSTER #6:
YOU ARE LETTING YOUR KIDS BLOCK MARITAL INTIMACY

This sex buster can be summarized in one word: Kids. Now, I believe children are gifts from God. But kids can, and will, bust up your sex life. "K.I.D.S." stands for "Keeping Intimacy at a Distance Successfully."

If you are not having a regular date night, this sex buster can easily rear its ugly head. If you don't have regular, enforced bed times for your children and certain areas of the house that are restricted during your "romantic hours," your intimate times will be few and far between.

SEX BUILDER #6:
TAKE A ROMANTIC GETAWAY

I challenge you to take two breaks a year, just for the two of you. Get away for a night or two twice a year. Get away to fan the flames of romance. Get away for intimacy. Get away for sex.

Some people have the excuse, "You just don't know our finances. We can't afford that." What about camping? Maybe your family can step in to help you with the kids so you can have a little marital retreat at home.

Use creativity to make this happen because it is better to pay a small financial price now than to end up relationally bankrupt later on down the road. Taking these breaks is worth it and will reap huge benefits in your marriage.

9. What are some reasonably inexpensive retreats you have taken, or heard that others have taken?

_____

_____

_____

_____

SEX BUSTER #7:
YOU ARE SHARING SACRED STUFF WITH THE WRONG PEOPLE

Do not share those tidbits regarding what goes on in the bedroom with your golfing buddies, your tennis gal pals, or with the person next to you at work.

Marriage should be honored by all, and the marriage bed kept pure.... Hebrews 13:4

Talking with a trusted Christian counselor or pastoral counselor is one thing, but that's where it needs to stop. If you blab this sacred stuff all over the community, it will take away trust from your spouse and can even fan the flames of adultery.

SEX BUILDER #7:
DISCUSS SEX OPENLY WITH YOUR SPOUSE

The person you should be having a sex talk with is your spouse. Sit down and share your likes and dislikes, wants and desires, problems and needs. Put it on the table and deal with it in your marriage, not outside with strangers.

Maybe you need to go through a book on sex like "Restoring the Pleasure" by Drs. Cliff and Joyce Penner. You could read one chapter a night aloud together or separately. Then, each of you highlight your favorite passages to discuss later. You won't believe what can happen.

If you're uncomfortable talking about sexual matters openly, then start slowly until you can develop a mutual comfort level for heart-to-heart sharing. The greatest thing in sex is communication, so you need to find a way to bring communication into the marriage bed.

SEX BUSTER #8:
YOU ARE STUCK IN MONOTONY

You've heard about a monogamous relationship, right? That's a good thing. Well, there's something out there called a monotonous marriage that is not such a good thing. In fact, it's a big time sex buster.

This marriage consists of the same old, same old, rut-like relationship. You've got the same old look, wearing the same old wardrobe, talking the same old talk, stuck in the same old place, and engaged in the same old love making.

10. What are common areas in a marriage where monotony can set in?

_____

_____

_____

_____

Instead of monotony, we need to model our lives and relationships after the essence of God. God is not monotonous; he is highly creative and innovative. If we know him, live for him and worship him corporately and individually, we are going to have creativity in every area of our lives—including sex.

SEX BUILDER #8:
BRING BACK THE ROMANCE

If you look up the word "impractical" in the dictionary, one of the synonyms is "romantic." Don't you like that? We have to become impractical people of romance.

Guys, we need help here. Here is your challenge, men. Take a modern translation of the Bible and read the Old Testament book, "The Song of Solomon." This is some seriously hot stuff! It is written to husbands and wives concerning lovemaking and how to keep romance in a relationship.

Solomon was creative. Solomon made his wife earrings. Solomon wrote her poetry. Solomon paneled the master bedroom by himself with fine wood cut from the cedars of Lebanon. And he took her on long walks through the forest.

What did his wife do? Did she respond to his creativity with monotony? No, she didn't. She approached him the way he wanted to be approached.

The text reads that she danced before him in a sheer negligee. It says that Solomon took her to a biblical Bed and Breakfast. Solomon's wife took the initiative and said to him, "Solomon, let's make love outdoors. I want to show you something old and something new."

I'll stop there. You can read the rest for yourself.

11. Husbands, tell your wives some scenarios that you think are romantic.

12. Wives, tell your husbands some scenarios that you think are romantic.

WRAP IT UP

When we started today, I asked what you think about when you hear the word sex. It is my prayer that from now on you will think about God and the biblical connotations Lisa and I have outlined in this chapter. God wants you to do sex his way, stay within his parameters and use this amazing gift the way he desires. Thank God for that desire for the opposite sex. Let's build great sex into our marriages by following these sex builders and eliminating those sex busters. And most of all, have fun!

Prayer Requests:

_____

_____

_____

_____

_____

_____

Notes:

_____

_____

_____

_____

_____

_____

_____

_____

STEP IT UP

Take a step further over the next few days and spend some time reflecting on the following devotional thoughts that reinforce the previous session. Use these as reminders to take what you've learned and apply it to your everyday life.

DAY 1

Read Genesis 2:24

God is the creator of sex and he created humans as sexual beings. In an attempt to draw us away from God, though, the enemy tries to use our healthy desire for sex to lure us into sin. He has used various venues to poison people's attitudes and understanding of sex. Movies, television, and popular opinion today rarely reflect any of the ideas about sex that God intends. Most people don't even know that God cares about their sexual relationship with their spouse. But he does.

Research shows that one-third to one-half of married couples experience a moderate to major level of sexual frustration. God does not intend for us to suffer frustration in our sexual relationship with our spouse. The first biblical account of marriage refers to husbands and wives becoming "one flesh." This is a reference to one of the results of physical intimacy in marriage.

Marital intimacy is the physical manifestation of the spiritual connection between a husband and wife, and it is a critical element in the success of every marriage.

Do you feel that your sexual relationship with your spouse is creating more connection or conflict?

If conflict, why do you think there is conflict, and what could you do to be a part of the solution?

Notes:

_____

_____

_____

_____

_____

_____

_____

_____

Prayer Requests:

_____

_____

_____

_____

_____

_____

_____

_____

_____

_____

_____

DAY 2

Read 1 Corinthians 7:3-4

Scripture tells us that our bodies belong not only to ourselves, but that we share them jointly with our spouse. They are community property. If your marriage is healthy, you don't prohibit one another from having free access to every room in your house. The same is true with your body. Wives have full access to their husband's body and husbands have full access to their wife's body.

The key here is that we have to respect one another in the process. We must seek to understand our spouse's sex drive in order to have a sensational sexual relationship. We all know men and women are wired up differently.

Generally speaking, men have a greater sex drive and can go from zero to sixty, sexually, in a matter of seconds. Women, on the other hand, generally don't have as strong of a sex drive and they enter into sex at a much mellower pace. In order to respect your rights to your spouse's body, you have to respect their sex drive.

Husbands, how do you need to change the way you approach your wife when it comes to your sexual intimacy?

Wives, how can you better respect your husband's sex drive?

Notes:

_____

_____

_____

_____

_____

_____

_____

_____

Prayer Requests:

_____

_____

_____

_____

_____

_____

_____

_____

_____

_____

_____

DAY 3

Read Job 31:1 and James 1:5

A covenant is like a contract on steroids with God as the judge. It outlines the rights, responsibilities, and actions between two parties in advance of an occurrence. Job made a covenant with his eyes so that he knew in advance what he would do when faced with sexual temptation. Why was Job so intent on keeping his eyes pure? Because he understood sin's progression, which is illustrated in James 1:5.

Both Job and James understood the idea that if we wait for lust to tempt us, it is too late. We have to be prepared if we are to act appropriately in the face of sexual temptation. Looking lustfully at others steals the satisfaction and enchantment that we have with the spouse God has given us.

Do you want a cold marriage in which you are bored and frustrated? Or do you want a marriage in which you are forever satisfied with your spouse's sexuality? Make a covenant with your eyes not to look lustfully at anyone other than your spouse and discover the amazing sexual life God has in store for you in your marriage.

Notes:

_____

_____

_____

_____

_____

_____

_____

_____

Prayer Requests:

_____

_____

_____

_____

_____

_____

_____

_____

_____

_____

_____

DAY 4

Read Hebrews 13:4

We have all heard the saying, "Gentlemen don't kiss and tell." Well, according to the Bible, this is a sound policy for both ladies and gentlemen.

There is a quiet, but destructive force unleashed when we share the intimate details of our sex life with anyone other than our spouse. You may not notice the waves of destruction immediately, but they inevitably crash against the shores of your marriage, eroding your trust and confidence in one another.

If you want to talk about sex, do so with your spouse. Communication is a key to satisfying sex. Let your husband or wife know your likes and dislikes, your desires, wants and needs. If this is uncomfortable for you, it might be a good idea to read a Christian book on sex together. You may need to start your discussions slowly and build a comfort level over time. No matter what you do, though, do not violate the trust you share by telling others about what happens in your marriage bed.

How well do you guard your marriage bed by not relating its secrets to your buddies or girlfriends?

Notes:

_____

_____

_____

_____

_____

_____

_____

_____

Prayer Requests:

_____

_____

_____

_____

_____

_____

_____

_____

_____

_____

DAY 5

Read 1 Corinthians 7:5

The Bible never says how often a husband and wife should be physically intimate. It does, though, tell us that it is unhealthy for a couple to abstain from sex for an extended period of time. The break in physical intimacy only allows Satan to infiltrate the marriage with temptation.

This passage does give one specific reason to abstain for a time, but both husband and wife must agree. The one reason is prayer. Praying together draws you together with your spouse emotionally and spiritually. This emotional and spiritual connection will, in turn, lead you back to a time of physical connection.

If you are consistently too tired or too busy for sex with your spouse, consider the words the Apostle Paul penned to the Corinthians generations ago. They are still applicable today, perhaps more than ever.

What could you do to make sure the principle from this verse is a part of your marriage?

Notes:

_____

_____

_____

_____

_____

_____

_____

_____

Prayer Requests:

_____

_____

_____

_____

_____

_____

_____

_____

_____

_____

_____

CREATIVE FINANCES

CREATIVE MARRIAGE

START IT UP

I'll never forget the first time I mowed the backyard of our first house. After mowing some pretty straight lines through our lawn and making it about half way through the yard, it happened. I found myself suddenly ambushed by hundreds of bees!

In the midst of the ensuing chaos that you are probably familiar with, I was stung three times. Now that might not sound so bad, but I am allergic to bees. Needless to say, I wanted to avoid being stung again. So I began the dance we all know. When that didn't work, I tucked tail, ran inside and yelled, "Lisa! Bees ... everywhere ... stinging ...allergic!"

Over the next several hours, Lisa and I did all we could think of to get rid of the bees. Finally, after failing miserably, we decided to call a man who specializes in outdoor pest control—Mr. Smith.

We explained to Mr. Smith that we had an angry hive of bees in a tree house, and we asked him what to do. He advised us to calm down and said he would be right over to handle the situation. He said, "I have dealt with bees for the last fifteen years. Bees won't sting me, because I know their habits. And I have this special concoction that will wipe them out."

Mr. Smith came right over and climbed up the tree house to get a better evaluation of the "situation." Immediately, the bees attacked. Mr. Smith was caught off guard and fell off the ladder. Thankfully he was okay, but the bees were on the attack again.

After finally getting control of the situation, Mr. Smith told us that these bees were the nastiest ones he had seen in his fifteen year career. They were so aggressive, in fact, that we sent them off Texas A & M to see if they were killer bees.

1. Describe the worst bite or sting you have received?

_____

_____

_____

_____

TALK IT UP

Being attacked by bees is definitely frightening. But there is something out there that is even scarier—killer fees. It doesn't matter if you make billions, millions, thousands or hundreds of dollars; if you are married, you are going to be attacked in one form or another by these killer fees.

Gallop estimates that fifty-six percent of divorces every year in our country are due to conflict and arguments over finances. It is a major problem and a major source of conflict in marriage. So, just like hunting down the source of a bee hive to kill the bees, the first thing we need to do to protect our finances is to discover the source of these killer fees.

ATTACK OF THE PLASTIC PIRANHAS

The first source of attack is in the form of plastic. You know what I'm talking about—credit cards. You get married and begin to use credit cards to buy certain "necessary" items. You know, that special blender for your kitchen and that high-definition television for your living room. When this type of spending becomes a regular habit, the killer fees are buzzing close by.

Credit cards are interesting little cards. They come in pretty, shiny colors of red, white, blue, gold, and platinum. You can buy beautiful nature pictures or have your favorite college team plastered all over the card. They even have our names engraved on the bottom of the card and tell how long we have been "members."

2. Think back to your early credit card days. How old were you when you first got a credit card and how well did you use your credit card?

_____

_____

_____

_____

3. Do a wallet check now. How many credit cards do you have in your wallet?

_____

_____

_____

_____

As you go on your merry way through life with credit cards, you're thinking to yourself, "A credit card is the way to go. I love this little card. It's my friend."

However, thirty days later, you bring in the mail and you hear a muffled sound of chomping and chewing. And when you open up the envelope and look at the bill in your hand, the persistent sound becomes obvious. It is the precursor to an imminent attack by the killer fees. You are being stalked by the dreaded plastic piranhas. And they smell blood.

The credit card companies have realized that we all know what is coming. So they have tried to convince us that when we sign up for their special, zero interest card, that we are avoiding the imminent attack. But don't be deceived.

Introductory rate or not, credit cards will get you in the end, because most of us use credit cards to buy things with money we do not have. Studies show that Americans who have credit cards spend twenty-six percent more than those who don't.

The borrower is servant to the lender. Proverbs 22:7

Money can easily become a slave trader, selling us up the river to a lender who gains mastery over us.

4. How can debt make you feel enslaved?

_____

_____

_____

_____

Basically, we have two options with credit cards. And I want to challenge you to apply these options. The first option is to pay them off every month. Credit cards should be a tool of convenience, not a financial mechanism for getting what we can't afford to pay cash for.

The second option is more drastic, but necessary for many of us. Take a pair of scissors and cut up your credit cards. Some of you need to get serious about this because your finances are out-of-control.

I have heard people say, "Well, the Bible says time and time again never to borrow money."

The Bible doesn't tell us to never borrow money. What the Bible does speak against is borrowing money and not being able to pay it back. We should be cautious borrowers by borrowing as little as possible, only when absolutely necessary, and only when we can pay it back.

The wicked borrow and do not repay.... Psalm 37:21

5. Why do you think God describes those who do not repay what they borrow as "wicked"?

_____

_____

_____

_____

6. How does God's view of debt differ from what is communicated by society as a whole?

_____

_____

_____

_____

There is no kind of pressure that compares to being under the gun financially. So don't let debt spin out-of-control, because debt will begin to rule and run your life. If those plastic piranhas in your wallet are attacking you, then it's time to fight back.

THE MEDIA BLITZ

Another source of the killer fees is the media. The American Association of Advertising estimates that the average person in our society sees or hears over 7,000 commercials or advertisements per day.

Advertisers hire the best producers, the best writers, and the best actors to participate in these commercials with one goal in mind: to create discontent. They want the viewer to say, "I have to have that," or, "I need to buy that," or, "I can't live without that."

7. Who do you think has some of the most effective advertisements?

_____

_____

_____

_____

Advertising is a multi-billion dollar industry because it works. They are succeeding in creating discontent in our society, even among Christians who should know that contentment can't be purchased at a department store.

> Behold, I send you out as sheep in the midst of wolves. Therefore be wise as serpents and harmless as doves. Matthew 10:16

8. How could you be wise when you see tempting advertisements?

_____

_____

_____

_____

When you see a commercial, let me challenge you to look at the un-pictured, hidden side of the commercial.

For example, let's consider a beer commercial. One of the classics features a guy with about three percent body fat who drives his $70,000 shiny sports car up to this quaint little yuppie bar and steps out.

What this slick commercial is not showing you is the hidden reality of the alcohol abuse that can often occur. It doesn't show that same guy after he orders 10 beers and then crashes his shiny sports car into a telephone pole—or worse, another car. It also conveniently leaves out the health risks associated with alcohol abuse or the fact that his car costs more than he can really afford.

Whenever you watch a commercial, train yourself to look at the unspoken side of what they're selling. Don't allow yourself to be deceived.

THE PEER PRESSURE PRESS

A third source of the killer fees is peer pressure. I like the word peer, because it communicates a word picture of peering at each other to see what the other person has.

"They have that home. They drive that car. They are members of that club. I am just as educated, I'm just as smart, and I'm just as young. I deserve it as much as they do!"

9. Describe a time you did something you would not have done without peer pressure.

_____

_____

_____

_____

Peer pressure can even happen in your home. Take Al, the average American child. As Al grows up during his impressionable years, most of the conversation he hears around the breakfast table centers on money, what it can get, what it can buy. So Al comes to the conclusion that money really does talk.

Al watches his parents get rewarded for climbing the corporate ladder. He sees the importance money plays in his family, so he begins to think money is the most important thing in the world. The advice he gets on his future is, "Find a college that will set you up to get the job that pays the most."

Al graduates, gets involved in a high-power career, makes a lot of money, gets married and begins to pass on, unknowingly and unwittingly, this same value system that he learned from his parents to his own children.

As an elderly man, he looks back over his life and discovers that his whole life has been focused on the pursuit of money. He has been led around through life on a short leash, oblivious to the struggles it caused in his life. Sadly, money played a larger role in his life than the things that should have mattered the most.

Unfortunately, this example is common in today's world. Far too many people, including Christians, are being led around by this materialistic, money-driven mentality.

THE BUDGET BLOCKADE

How do we take care of these methods of attack? How do we fend off the plastic piranha? How do we dodge the media blitz? How do we hold up under the peer pressure press? It is spelled B-U-D-G-E-T. We need to address the importance of a budget, because the Bible says that we should live on and follow a budget.

First, when you set a budget, pray about it with your spouse. Everything we have comes from God, so God needs to be involved in every decision regarding our resources.

So pray, "God, where do you want us to spend our money? What do you want us to do? Where do you want us to put limits and where do you want us to be generous?"

Also, set some mutual goals. Agree together about some goals for saving, for spending and for giving. To make it easy, you should live by the give-give-live budget.

FIRST THINGS FIRST

The first give in the budget is setting aside at least ten percent of everything you make for the local church. The Bible is plain about this concept. We are commanded to bring this first ten percent to our local house of worship. It is called tithing.

> *Honor the LORD with your wealth, with the firstfruits of all your crops; then your barns will be filled to overflowing, and your vats will brim over with new wine. Proverbs 3:9-10*

The amount you make is insignificant. If you make a million dollars a month or if you make ten dollars a month, the Bible says that the first ten percent should go to God.

God doesn't need our money. He wants our heart. And he knows that when we are faithful and bring back to him what is already his, we are admitting that he is Lord of all in our lives.

When we hoard our money and refuse to follow this simple command, we are showing God and others that we think we are the master of our own domain.

10. If you tithe, how has it positively affected your life?

_____

_____

_____

_____

Anyone can look at your financial portfolio and tell what is number one in your life. Is it travel? Is it clothing? Is it a home? Is it a car? Or is it the Lord Jesus Christ?

When you get paid, give the first ten percent to God. It will bless your life, your marriage, and your family in ways that you can't even imagine.

THE PERSONAL PAYBACK

The second give in the budget is giving ourselves the next ten percent. I'm talking about the biblical concept of saving money.

> In the house of the wise are stores of choice food and oil, but a foolish man devours all he has. Proverbs 21:20

> Go to the ant, you sluggard; consider its ways and be wise! It has no commander, no overseer or ruler, yet it stores its provisions in summer and gathers its food at harvest. Proverbs 6:6-8

Have you ever seen fire ants? Fire ants are interesting creatures, and you would do well to just take a step back (a big step back), and watch the fire ants.

The wise fire ant gathers and saves stuff, but it does not have a leader, a CEO or a coach. Yet, the fire ant lives wisely on less than it gathers and puts the rest away for a later time—when the gathering will not be as easy.

I read recently that the average European saves sixteen percent of his annual income. The average Japanese man or woman saves twenty-five percent of their annual income. The average American saves only four percent of their annual income. As Americans in a materialistic society, we need to tone down the consumerism and tune into a saving and investment mentality.

11. What are some of the common reasons for not saving more?

_____

_____

_____

_____

12. What are some strategies that could help you either start saving or start saving more?

_____

_____

_____

_____

As you begin to save and invest, you will learn the principle of contentment. The Bible says over and over again that when we live God's way, we will experience contentment. We should be content with the contents of our life.

THE ENJOYMENT FACTOR

God loves to give us gifts. But we need to be wise with those gifts. We need to say, "God, I want to live on a margin, so here is my budget. I'm giving the first ten percent to you and the second ten percent to myself." And then, the remaining eighty percent is what you get to enjoy.

Don't fall into the mindset that prevents you from enjoying what God has blessed you with. Don't feel guilty if you are financially blessed. God says that you can live where you want to live, drive what you want to drive, and wear what you want to wear—as long as you are faithful in bringing the tithe and saving at least ten percent. Because when you live by God's guidelines, there will be money left for you to enjoy. So live it up!

13. How do you think applying the give, give, live principle could help you enjoy the money you spend?

_____

_____

_____

_____

WRAP IT UP

Money is not the root of all kinds of evil. The Bible says that the love of money is. Money itself is neutral. The question is, do you own your money or does your money own you?

It is my prayer that God's principles of budgeting will become the gauge in your financial life. Because if you will apply these biblical principles, God can and will do great things in all areas of your marriage and personal life.

Prayer Requests:

_____

_____

Notes:

_____

_____

_____

STEP IT UP

Take a step further over the next few days and spend some time reflecting on the following devotional thoughts that reinforce the previous session. Use these as reminders to take what you've learned and apply it to your everyday life.

DAY 1

Read Proverbs 24:3-4

You might be thinking, "What does money have to do with marriage?" Well, it is a major issue in marriage. A Gallup poll estimates that fifty-six percent of divorces every year in our country are due to conflicts about finances.

Over the next several days we will be looking at several biblical principles that will guide our family finances. We need to start by getting a good dose of God's wisdom.

We all need God's wisdom to build our house. We need his understanding to establish our home. We need godly knowledge to fill your rooms. If we lack wisdom in the financial area of your marriage, we need to go to God for the answers.

Ask God to start showing you his wisdom for your finances.

Notes:

_____

_____

_____

_____

_____

_____

_____

_____

Prayer Requests:

_____

_____

_____

_____

_____

_____

_____

_____

_____

_____

DAY 2

Read Proverbs 22:7

Nothing gets us in financial quicksand faster than credit cards. Studies show that Americans who have credit cards spend twenty-six percent more than those who do not. When we buy things on credit we are basically spending money we don't have. For a while it feels good, but the bill always comes due.

It is tempting to just pay the minimum balance due, but the interest begins to really pile up. As this cycle continues we become slaves to our credit card debt. And the lenders become masters over us!

Are you a slave to debt? Is credit card debt keeping you in financial bondage? Is the monthly juggling act getting you down?

Ask God to help you control your credit card spending. Ask for his wisdom in developing a plan to get out of debt bondage.

Do a credit card count. How many credit cards do you have that are not paid off on a monthly basis?

Remember, the goal is to have zero.

Notes:

_____
_____
_____
_____
_____
_____
_____
_____

Prayer Requests:

_____
_____
_____
_____
_____
_____
_____
_____
_____
_____

DAY 3

Read Psalm 37:21

In yesterday's devotional, we looked at the problems created by excessive debt, especially credit card debt. But the Bible never says that we should not borrow money. When I hear people say "Well, the Bible says time and time again never to borrow money," I know right away they haven't read the book.

What the Bible does talk about is borrowing money and not being able to pay it back. God has harsh words for the person who does not pay his debts. In fact, he calls them wicked.

We should be cautious borrowers by borrowing as little as possible, only when absolutely necessary, and only when we can pay it back.

Evaluate your borrowing habits and ask God to guide your borrowing decisions—both long-term and short-term.

Notes:

_____

_____

_____

_____

_____

_____

_____

_____

Prayer Requests:

_____

_____

_____

_____

_____

_____

_____

_____

_____

_____

DAY 4

Read Matthew 6:21

How we spend our money says a lot about our spiritual condition. The way we use our money reveals where our heart is. Jesus says that where your treasure is, so is our commitment, attention and affection.

There is something strange about money. People who might share other parts of their lives freely have a hard time sharing their money. Those who can make quick decisions in all other areas sometimes struggle to make wise decisions about money. Money has a special place in our lives; and it can be a dangerous place if we are not careful.

We can look at our financial portfolios and our check registers and easily tell what is number one in our lives. Look at your bank statement. What does it say about where your heart is?

Notes:

_____

_____

_____

_____

_____

_____

_____

_____

_____

Prayer Requests:

_____

_____

_____

_____

_____

_____

_____

_____

_____

_____

_____

_____

DAY 5

Read Philippians 4:11-12

This week we talked about the principles of stewardship and how these principles should impact our finances. Think back to last week's study and the Give-Give-Live principle.

God didn't give us these principles because he is a cosmic killjoy. Rather, he gives us these principles because he knows that the stress and strain of financial burdens has sunk many marriages and he doesn't want that to happen in our marriages.

One of the greatest benefits of living by these principles is contentment. Read what the Apostle Paul says in today's passage again.

Paul learned that contentment was a two-sided coin. He learned to be content with what he had and what he didn't have. When we're content, we won't be tempted to borrow in excess, spend compulsively, or abuse credit.

How is your contentment level? Ask the Lord to develop contentment in your life.

Notes:

_____

_____

_____

_____

_____

_____

_____

_____

Prayer Requests:

_____

_____

_____

_____

_____

_____

_____

_____

_____

_____

_____

CREATIVE MARRIAGE

CREATIVE PRIORITIES

START IT UP

It was a simple, passing comment made early one morning in a local coffee shop. A toddler-toting mom was sitting in a comfortable chair talking to another woman about being a wife and a parent.

I was sitting just a few feet away, studying and doing some research on marriage and family issues, so I said, "Excuse me. I'm doing some research on marriage and parenting. Would you mind if I ask you a couple of questions?"

They said, "Sure." So I began to ask them a little about their particular situations. After just a few questions, these two women began to open up and share some of their deepest concerns about marriage and parenting.

After a while, it was time for me to head to the office, so I packed up my briefcase and headed out of the shop. But just as I reached the door, the toddler-toting mom turned, looked at me, and made the statement that I will not soon forget. She said, "You know, I think I'm a great mom, but not that good of a wife."

1. Do you think some people are wired to be only a good spouse or a good parent?

_____

_____

_____

_____

2. Explain whether you think it is easier to be a good spouse or a good parent. Why do you feel this way?

_____

_____

_____

_____

As I thought about the statement that woman made in the coffee shop, it occurred to me that a lot of parents today would echo that same frustration. I think many would say, "You know, I'm getting the parental job done pretty well. But the spouse thing still needs a lot of work."

I believe it is critical that we understand the tension expressed in this statement if we are going to have the kind of marriages God wants us to have.

TALK IT UP

"Should my home be a kid-centric home? Should all of the activities and scheduling revolve around my children? Or should my family be a spouse-centric unit where the marriage takes precedence, where the marriage is the ultimate priority? Which one do I put first?"

This kid-centric family has become a popular idea in modern American society. And its effects have had tornado-like devastation on families from coast-to-coast. But the funnel cloud didn't just appear—it began forming during the sixties and the seventies.

After World War II and the baby boom, well-meaning parents turned their backs on the Bible and turned their backs on the advice from their parents; and instead, they put their parental stock in people like Dr. Spock. I'm not talking about the man of _Star Trek®_ fame. I'm talking about the man of permissive parenting fame.

Dr. Spock and other permissive parenting persuaders said, "The home should be a democratic institution. Everybody is equal. There's no real leader."

And these "experts" urged parents to crawl into the playpens with their rebellious toddlers, sit Indian-style next to them, and try to reason with them. And it all sounded so vogue, so hip, so cool, so modern. And liberated parents everywhere bought into this philosophy hook, line, and sinker.

3. Do you think the average parent today is better, the same, or worse than parents in the 1950's? Explain your opinion.

_____

_____

_____

_____

But the permissive parenting style has some major flaws. All you have to do is go to a restaurant with a kid-centric family to see those flaws up close and personal. But here's what happens when you put your child at the center of your solar system and revolve everything around him or her.

Let's say that a young couple, who are deeply in love, gets married. Then they have a few kids. The wife steps down from her number one priority—that of being a wife—and becomes a mom first. In essence, she marries her children.

Conversely, the husband steps down from his number one priority—that of being a husband—and marries his career. Now he chases promotions and money.

For the wife to get to her husband, she has to negotiate through a maze of work responsibilities and meetings. For the husband to get to his wife, he has to negotiate around all the needs, and the greeds, of the children.

The ramifications of this shift in priorities are numerous and costly. You have marital drift taking place as you begin to lose touch—emotionally, spiritually, and physically—with the person you married. It can seem like you are merely sharing a house as roommates, rather than sharing lives in a one-flesh relationship.

This funnel cloud of the kid-centric homes has been picking up speed over the past several decades and is now almost spinning out of control. Families today are cranking out rebellious, selfish, sassy, irresponsible children. And, sadly, the same funnel cloud has been leaving wrecked marriage after wrecked marriage in its wake.

This was not God's design for the family. Yes, we are to love our kids. We want the best for them. But we must understand that making our children the center of the family universe is not in their best interest, and it is certainly not in the best interest of the marriage relationship.

From the very beginning in Genesis, the obvious scriptural priority in the family unit is the marriage. Marriage must take priority over every relationship, including our relationship with our children.

4. What do you think the average parent would say if you asked them for a definition of parenting?

_____

_____

_____

_____

I want to share with you my working definition of parenting:

Parenting is the process of teaching and training your children to leave.

I didn't pull this definition out of thin air. It comes straight from the principles found in God's Word regarding parenting. Let's pull apart this definition and look at each facet of our God-given responsibility as parents.

TEACH -

These commandments that I give you today are to be upon your hearts. Impress them on your children. Talk about them when you sit at home and when you walk along the road, when you lie down and when you get up. Tie them as symbols on your hands and bind them on your foreheads. Write them on the doorframes of your houses and on your gates. Deuteronomy 6:6-9

TRAIN -

Train a child in the way he should go, and when he is old he will not turn from it. Proverbs 22:6

CHILDREN LEAVE -

For this reason a man will leave his father and mother and be united to his wife, and they will become one flesh. Genesis 2:24

Children are supposed to leave and parents are supposed to stay. Thus, the marriage should be at the top of the family food chain.

Have you ever wondered why there are so many twenty-somethings and even thirty-somethings still living at home? It's because their families have been kid-centric for so long, they've felt the warm spotlight for so long, and they have been in the starring role for so long, they don't want to leave.

The parents are doing all the work and the children are getting all the perks. And when the kids turn eighteen, they say to themselves, "Hey, this is a sweet deal! I get a free room, free laundry service, and incredible meals. Plus, I can work, make a salary, and have a lot of money to spend."

And the kid-centric family funnel cloud keeps building strength.

5. What do you think keeps so many parents from putting the marriage at the top of the family food chain?

_____

_____

_____

_____

Have you thought about the fact that you will have approximately eighteen years with your children, but you will have the rest of your life with your spouse? You are not benefiting anyone by focusing on the kids to the detriment of your marriage relationship.

If you are not parenting your children to leave, you are missing the boat with them. And if you are not nurturing your marital relationship, you are drifting away from the one person with whom you will be spending the rest of your life. You are facing the very real prospect of living out your post-parenting years in a home with a person you don't know anymore.

If you want to build a mutually satisfying marriage and be a great parent at the same time, your relationship with your spouse must come first. After all, the Bible compares Christ's love for the church to a husband's love for his wife. Children aren't mentioned. Friends are not used in the comparison.

I love my children and I know you love yours. But as a husband or wife, your focus should be on the marriage, because everything else in the home flows from that biblical priority.

So how do we maintain a spouse-centric household? In order to attain the ultimate destination for our marriages and families, we must take a journey through several destinations.

ATTENTIONVILLE

The first destination is a place called "Attentionville." Let me ask you a question: Do children need oxygen? Sure they do. But if you give them too much oxygen, it will smother them.

Do children need attention? Sure they do. But if you give too much attention to them, it will smother them as well.

Kid-centric families are in danger of smothering their kids. But for our kids to thrive, we must balance the attention we give them with the attention we need to give to the marriage relationship.

Lisa and I made the choice several years ago to make our family spouse-centric. Here's how it plays out: I usually arrive home by 5:30 or 6:00 pm. I walk in the door, greet the kids by giving them kisses and hugs. Then, Lisa and I will spend some time talking in the kitchen—alone. If one of the kids comes in to interrupt, I'll turn and say, "For the next twenty or thirty minutes, don't come into the kitchen. Your mother and I are going to talk. Now, if there's bloodshed, come in. Other than that, go and play."

Sometimes they'll cry or moan because they want my attention. But I believe this kind of routine teaches them that Mommy comes first to Daddy, and spending time with her is Daddy's number one priority. It also teaches them autonomy and responsibility. It teaches them how to separate and individuate. It communicates in a real-life way, "The marriage is the most important aspect of this family."

6. What are some other ways you can make time with your spouse the number priority in your home?

_____

_____

_____

_____

Don't miss the importance of this first destination. Attentionville is a place you need to travel through, but it is not a place where you set up camp. Our kids need us to spend a certain amount of time with them everyday, in balance with the time you spend with your spouse. I'm all for children. I love to spend time with mine. But we have to do it in a scheduled manner. You don't have to set up some militaristic, ultra-strict schedule, but certain time increments must be maintained if you are going to achieve the proper balance of a spouse-centric household.

NIGHT-NIGHT-VILLE

There's another destination we need to travel through in order to create a spouse-centric household, and I have written a song to illustrate this special place.

Let's all go to Night-night-ville.
There we will get very still.
It's time to go to Night-night-ville.
So everyone needs to chill.

Now, this song is not that popular around our household, but Night-night-ville is the next destination we must travel through on a daily basis. This doesn't just mean getting your kids to bed whenever they get tired or feel like going to bed. To maintain the balance of a spouse-centric home, there needs to be a structured and patterned bedtime.

Set up a routine for putting your children to bed every night. You can spend time reading Bible stories and praying. Make sure it is understood that after reading or bath time or whatever routine you have, it's time for lights out.

And here's the kicker. This established time is not for their benefit; it's for your benefit! Don't put them down when they're ready. Put them down when you're ready. Take a step back and ask, "Okay, how much time do we need as a married couple to connect at night?" Then do the math and put the kids down early enough for you to connect.

7. What could be some of the obstacles of instituting "Night-night-ville," and how can you overcome those obstacles?

_____

_____

_____

_____

When our twins were five and our son was eight, Lisa and I put them to bed between 7:30 and 7:45. That may sound pretty early to you—they could have stayed up later than that—but we established this time for our benefit, not theirs. As they get older, we reevaluate their bedtime and let them stay up a little later. Even though they are getting older, they still need that structured time of rest, and we still need that time together in the evening as husband and wife.

To our teenager we would say, "LeeBeth, you can stay up until 10:00 or 10:15, but at about 9:00 we want you to head to your room and stay there until bedtime." It shows the priority of the spouse-centric family. It says that Mom and Dad have something special going on. It's very tempting to let your teenager set his or her own schedule, but you need to maintain control while at the same time giving them some freedom and flexibility.

Now, let's assume you've done that. You've had a few navigational errors, but you have finally arrived in Night-night-ville. This is not an easy thing, so you should be congratulated for arriving at this important family milestone. Yet, even with the kids in bed and no distractions, something may be keeping you from maximizing this exclusive time together.

Do you remember the infamous "Love Bug" virus that attacked computers all over the globe several years ago? The front page of *USA Today* reported: "FBI hunts Love Bug source. Damage from e-mail virus cuts across USA and worldwide. A worldwide hunt is on to find the source of the Love Bug computer virus that jammed e-mail systems Thursday from Asia to California."

Well, there's another virus that's worse than the Love Bug virus. It's the marital Love Bug virus and it's also affecting homes from Asia to California.

Here's how it happens. Say you have put your kids to bed and you finally have a little free time, a little quiet time, so you decide to make a few phone calls. The telephone is one of the major avenues for the Marital Love Bug to attack your home. Keep your phone calls to a minimum during this time so you can concentrate on connecting with your spouse.

Something else that causes this virus is housework and office work done in the home. Now and then there are some exceptions, but for the most part you should not use up this quality time finishing up chores or doing work. If you do, make an agreement with your spouse that you will each spend an hour or so doing some work, then devote the rest of the evening to each other.

The next way that the Marital Love Bug gets into your home seems to be the most benign. Many couples spend their evenings with the television remote between them, all the while thinking they are spending time with each other. "We just watch TV together, Ed. That's what we do."

But when the two of you are staring at an electronic box of two dimensional moving pictures, how much time are you really devoting to your spouse? How much communication is really happening?

Don't let the Marital Love Bug attack your marriage. Instead, use the routine of Night-night-ville to strengthen your marriage.

8. What could you do to overcome the Marital Love Bug virus?

_____

_____

_____

_____

As you consider the importance of Attentionville and Night-night-ville, consider the words of 1 Corinthians 14:40.

But everything should be done in a fitting and orderly way.

You must be committed to regular, scheduled time with your spouse or it won't happen. If you are not proactive about this, the kids will vie for all of your attention, the Marital Love Bug will bite, and you will discover one day that you have drifted apart from the one you vowed to spend your life with.

DATEVILLE

Let's travel to another location, Dateville. I've been talking about this particular destination for years now, and you will find me hammering this concept over and over again throughout this study.

I encourage couples to date at least twice a month. I'm referring to a date where you and your spouse go out—alone. This is the single greatest thing Lisa and I have done for our marriage!

You may be thinking, "Yeah, that sounds great in theory, but what about the real world? We've got schedules to compete with, finances to balance, and work and school to think about."

I can attest to the fact that it's not just a good theory; it can be done. Don't put it off. Hire a babysitter. Just have a standing sitter for a certain night. Or, if you don't want to do that, trade off childcare with some friends.

And the date does not have to be at night. A good friend of mine has "day-dates" with his wife. He has a day off in the middle of the week, so they have breakfast and lunch together and just spend time together during the day. Look at what works best for your schedule, and then be creative about making it fit. Now and again, you're going to have to fight some battles, but it is well worth the effort.

ACTIVITYVILLE

This next destination is probably the most difficult for families to negotiate, especially in today's fast-paced world—Activityville. We're burning our children out with soccer and baseball games and basketball practice and music lessons and cheerleading practice and voice lessons and dance recitals and art classes and...and...and....

Now, I'm all for extracurricular activities. I love athletics. I value art and dance. There is nothing wrong with kids being involved in competitive activities. But the keyword is balance.

9. When you were in elementary school, how many weeknights were occupied with out-of-the-house activities?

_____

_____

_____

_____

10. The schedules in most families today are dramatically busier than when we were children. What do you think are the benefits and the setbacks of these busy schedules?

_____

_____

_____

_____

A while back, my wife and I had dinner with a world class, multi-sport professional athlete. Over the appetizer portion of this meal together, this man looked at Lisa and me and said, "I will never let my children play children's athletics or get too involved in extracurricular activities. I want them to just enjoy being kids."

Now, I don't know if I'd go that far. Such a restriction is probably driven by some negative experiences from this man's own childhood. But I certainly understood where he was coming from. We need to allow children to be children, and over-scheduling them can take away from that carefree, childhood experience.

I'm not saying that children shouldn't be involved in any extracurricular activities. That's got to be your decision before God. But remember Jesus' powerful words when scheduling your children's activities.

But seek first his kingdom and his righteousness and all these things will be added to you. Matthew 6:33

Are you a Matthew 6:33 family? Can you keep your current pace of activities and sports and still maintain the priority of God in your family? That's the balance you need to achieve as you make your way through Activityville.

The pressures on the family are constant. We need to fight for our family by continuously evaluating our commitments against our priority of being a Matthew 6:33 family. When you make the decision to follow the right map toward the right destinations, you can look forward to reaching the ultimate destination of a loving and spouse-centric household.

The following quiz is designed to help you evaluate, in a practical way, how you are balancing the priorities of marriage and family. Answer each question as honestly and accurately as you can by circling the appropriate number (1-Never, 2-Sometimes, or 3-Always). Then, add up the answers and check your score in the scoring explanation included at the end of the quiz.

CREATIVE PRIORITIES BALANCED FAMILY TEST

1. Do you go on a date with your spouse at least twice a month?

Never   Sometimes   Always
1   2   3

2. Do you eat dinner as a family around the dinner table at least three times per week?

Never   Sometimes   Always
1   2   3

3. Do your children sleep in their own beds (not your bed)?

Never   Sometimes   Always
1   2   3

4. Do you and your spouse have TLC (Touch, Look, Conversation) on a daily basis?

Never   Sometimes   Always
1   2   3

5. Do you get away for a weekend alone as a couple (without your kids) at least twice a year?

Never   Sometimes   Always
1   2   3

6. Do you have sexual intimacy with your spouse at least two times a week?

Never   Sometimes   Always
1   2   3

7. Do you and your spouse present a unified front when your children question your authority?

Never   Sometimes   Always
1   2   3

8. Do you have a set bedtime for your kids/teens that is consistently enforced?

Never   Sometimes   Always
1   2   3

9. Do you regularly evaluate your calendar to prevent ECA-itis (over-scheduling Extra-Curricular Activities)?

Never   Sometimes   Always
1   2   3

10. Is weekly church attendance (age-appropriate worship/teaching) a priority for you and your children?

Never   Sometimes   Always
1   2   3

Total Score: _____

– If you scored 10-17, your marriage and family are way out of balance. Although you have good intentions, your priorities need a major tune up.

– If you scored 18-24, you are somewhat out of balance. As a married couple and as parents, you need to fine tune your priorities based on the principles from this chapter and throughout this book.

– If you scored 25-30, you have a balanced family. Continue to challenge yourself to follow God's design for your marriage and family.

WRAP IT UP

As the pastor of a growing church and a husband and father who has dedicated his life to the church and his family, I cannot stress enough the importance of the local church in the life of your marriage.

We intentionally ended the study with this critical issue because none of what we have talked about will be possible without the support of a local body of believers. The mutual encouragement, the service from and to others, the biblical accountability, and so many other aspects of the church are vitally important as you build and maintain your lives together.

And, even more fundamental, is the impact that the church will make on the lives of your children—now and forever.

If you don't take anything else away from this book, I would urge you to either find or stay connected to a church. And get involved. I know it can be uncomfortable at first, but the effort is well worth the eternal rewards. Discover God in a creative and dynamic environment where you can learn in very practical ways more about what it means to be a Christ-follower and enjoy a creative and lasting marriage!

Prayer Requests:

_____

_____

_____

_____

_____

_____

_____

_____

_____

Notes:

_____

_____

_____

_____

_____

_____

_____

_____

_____

_____

_____

STEP IT UP

Take a step further over the next few days and spend some time reflecting on the following devotional thoughts that reinforce the previous session. Use these as reminders to take what you've learned and apply it to your everyday life.

DAY 1

Read Ephesians 5:25

A husband's number one earthly priority is his wife. The Bible tells husbands to mirror Christ's love for the church in their marital relationship. This can be a very confusing concept.

How did Jesus love the church? He sacrificed everything, including his life, for her. He made the church's welfare his top priority and he devoted his days on earth to her care and development.

If every husband loved his wife like Christ loved the church, then every marriage would be great.

Husbands, are you loving your wives the way Christ loves the church?

Based on your answer to the previous question, make a plan for following Jesus' example of sacrificial love in your marriage.

CREATIVE MARRIAGE

Notes:

_____

_____

_____

_____

_____

_____

_____

_____

Prayer Requests:

_____

_____

_____

_____

_____

_____

_____

_____

_____

_____

_____

DAY 2

Read Ephesians 5:33

It is interesting that Paul, in his letter to the Ephesian church, told wives repeatedly to submit to their husbands and he told husbands repeatedly to love their wives. Why did he give us separate, specific instructions?

He looked at the society around him and saw women struggling to manage their newfound freedom in Christ. They were accustomed to being what we, today, would call second-class citizens, and they found the idea of submission unbearable. In the same way, men in ancient Rome were used to being the all-powerful leaders in their homes and did not see the need to treat women with respect or love.

Many people today are acting like the men and women of ancient Rome. They find submission an unbearable idea and see no reason to love or respect their spouse. Is submission sickening to you? Does the idea of sacrificially loving your spouse sound like too much to ask?

Pray for God to soften your heart. Pray that he will give you the grace and the strength to change your outlook about submitting and loving.

Notes:

_____

_____

_____

_____

_____

_____

_____

_____

Prayer Requests:

_____

_____

_____

_____

_____

_____

_____

_____

_____

_____

DAY 3

Read Deuteronomy 6:7

We have discovered that husbands and wives are to see their spouse as the number one priority in the family. But where do children fit in? How are moms and dads supposed to relate to their kids in an ever-changing family situation?

The Bible gives us some great direction on this by laying out a three part agenda for parents. The first part of this parenting plan is laid out in Deuteronomy 6:7. This verse tells parents that we are to be teachers. We should teach our children about God, Jesus, and the Bible.

If you have children, start a pattern of reading Bible stories to them, or with them, every night at bedtime. You will find many teachable moments and share invaluable time together.

If you do not have children at home, consider volunteering in your church's pre-school, children's, or youth ministries. You will be providing a great service not only to the kids, but also to the church.

Ask God to prepare you to teach the children he places in your life.

How often do you teach your children biblical principles?

Notes:

_____

_____

_____

_____

_____

_____

_____

_____

Prayer Requests:

_____

_____

_____

_____

_____

_____

_____

_____

_____

_____

_____

DAY 4

Read Proverbs 22:6

Yesterday we looked at part one of a three-part biblical parenting agenda. The second part of that agenda is for parents to train their children.

We should be preparing our children for the challenges and trials of life, training them to handle tough issues with Christian morals and ethics. The best way to train children is to model in your own life what you want them to do in theirs.

Start this training when your children are young. But even if they are older, it is never too late to begin training them up in the way they should go.

Consider what you are modeling for your kids. Do they see in you the image of Christ, or is it the world that you reflect?

Notes:

_____

_____

_____

_____

_____

_____

_____

_____

Prayer Requests:

_____

_____

_____

_____

_____

_____

_____

_____

_____

_____

_____

DAY 5

Read Matthew 6:33

Despite all of the differences in people's lives today, there is one thing that is constant. No matter who you are, where you live, what you do for a living, or how much money you have, there are 24 hours in every day. No more, no less. What a person chooses to do with those 24 hours defines their life.

The Bible tells us to seek God every day. It's supposed to be a priority. But all too often we don't leave time for seeking him. We schedule some activity into every waking moment of our lives and the lives of our children until there is simply no way to do everything. That is when we discover where our true priorities lie.

What gets cut? Is it the kids' weekend softball tournament? Or is it church? How about a night out with your friends or date night alone with your spouse? Which one is the higher priority in your life?

Look at your calendar, your to-do list, or whatever method of keeping track of daily activities you use. Are your activities centered on the priorities of God?

Parents, are your children's extracurricular activities taking too much time and wearing them (and you) out? Take some time to reprioritize your family's schedule to make your relationship with God the top priority. Because when you do, he will take every other area in your life to the next level!

Notes:

_____

_____

_____

_____

_____

_____

_____

_____

_____

Prayer Requests:

_____

_____

_____

_____

_____

_____

_____

_____

_____

_____

_____

CREATIVE FOUNDATION

LEADER'S NOTES

1. What are some of the most vibrant memories from your wedding day?

The day of your wedding can feel like one of the fastest days of your life. It starts with the final preparation for the ceremony. From there is time with groomsmen and bridesmaids. Then, the ceremony happens and it seems like everything happens at the speed of light until the moment you drive away from your reception.

Despite the speed of the day, there are moments that stick in the recesses of your mind. There are those images of the first time you see your soon to be spouse in full wedding attire. There are the moments of camaraderie with your friends who came to celebrate your relationship. There are those moments of joy with your family that stay with you.

2. What were a few of the most prevailing expectations for your marriage on that special day?

The marriage expectation bar can be set pretty high before the ceremony. There are expectations about communication and attention. There are expectations that this relationship will not run into the same obstacles as other couples. There is an expectation for the amount of sexual intimacy and it can be totally different depending on if you are the bride or the groom. Some expectations are reasonable; others end up showing you did not know as much as you thought.

3. Do you remember the vows you said on your wedding day? Use the blank space below to try to write out your wedding vows then compare what you wrote down with what others in the room remembered.

Tip: Not everyone makes the same vows so keep that in mind as you compare what was remembered. You may want to see if those who wrote their own vows could remember them better than those who used standard vows.

4. Brainstorm ideas for keeping your vows current in your marriage.

Keeping vows current starts with thinking about what was promised. This means going beyond just memorizing the words. How to fulfill those promises must be at the forefront of the mind. Then, once you know what to do, find ways to remember what you should do. This could be placing strategic notes, having friends encourage you, having evaluative talks with your spouse or reciting your vows on a regular basis. If you will practice this, you can keep your vows current.

5. What does God's willingness to take the initiative in our relationship with him communicate about his commitment?

It seems like the person who takes the initiative in a relationship is generally the most committed. Think back to early dating relationships. Most of the time, the person who was the most interested in the relationship called the most, wrote the most notes, asked when they could hang out... in general they took the initiative.

God showed his commitment to being in a relationship by showing love to the very people that sinned against him. God had every right to stay angry and punish his creation, yet he sacrificed so he could offer a road to forgiveness. If God was committed enough to overcome the first obstacle of sin by sacrificing his son, that shows he is committed enough to overcome any other obstacle.

6. How could you apply God's example of love to your marriage?

God took the initiative and made the necessary sacrifice to restore the relationship. When you feel frustrated with your spouse, when they have wronged you, when you have the right to be mad – remember how God loved you. Take the initiative with your spouse to restore the relationship.

7. Make a list of the most valuable things in your life. Then discuss the amount of work it takes to attain or maintain each of those valuable things.

Tip: Let the entire group brainstorm valuable things in their lives. Then, pick some of the most common answers to think about the work involved in attaining or maintaining those things. You may also compare the work to attain those things versus the work to maintain them. Which work was harder? Which work came more naturally? Which work was closer to your expectations?

8. When are some of the times it is most difficult to work at improving your marriage?

The obvious answer is that it is most difficult to work on improving your marriage when you are mad at your spouse. During those times, someone has to put their emotions aside and think about the other person.

It can also be difficult to work on your marriage when things are at their busiest. In the midst of many other activities and commitments it is easy to put your marriage on the back shelf. The idea is that your marriage is not going anywhere so you can always come back and work on it, but the other opportunities could fade at any moment. The truth is, there will always be other opportunities. But if you do not work on your marriage, it will not always be there.

One commonly overlooked time that can be difficult to work on your marriage is when things are going well. In those times of contentment, it is easy to become complacent and stop doing the things that got you to that place in your marriage.

9. What could you do to remind yourself that your work is not only for your spouse, it is for God?

Praying for your marriage can be a great way to remember the work is also for God. Thank God for the good parts of your marriage. In doing this you are acknowledging his involvement. Also, ask for his help. He does not expect you to fulfill your vows on your own strength. It is easy to get so wrapped up in fulfilling the marriage vows that God gets left out. By praying for your marriage you will keep God a part of your marriage and remember that your vows were to him as well.

10. What are some of the creative things you did for each other before you were married, or in the early days of your marriage?

Tip: Let the group discuss this question for a while. The goal is to inspire new ideas by listening to the ideas of the past. Hearing what was once done can be a great way to evaluate what is currently being done. When everyone is reminded of how much work they once put in, it can be a wake up call for the lack of effort now. Also, hearing the creative ideas can bring out the competitive side of the men. As they hear the women remember what was once done for them it can spur the men on to new actions.

One important part of this question is to not let it turn into a time of criticism for what is not being done. The goal is to show appreciation for what was done, not criticize what is not being done now. If this question turns into spouses attacking each other for a lack of creative effort, there is little chance creativity will come out of the conversation.

11. Why do you think God's characteristic of creativity gets ignored or moved down the priority list in marriage for other of God's characteristics?

Creativity is a characteristic of God that is overlooked in general. God's love, his commitment, grace and mercy seem to be what is keyed in on. The result is those characteristics are then emphasized in marriage. The problem is the Bible is permeating with examples of God's creativity. Creativity is constantly evident in his relationship with his creation. By noticing God's creativity in general, it will keep creativity from being ignored in the marriage.

CREATIVE NOTES

ICEBREAKERS

You're Invited

Before the first meeting in the *Creative Marriage* series, send out invitations to your small group that look like wedding invitations. Invite your group to learn how to have the creative marriage God desires for them.

BRIDGE – God invites us to experience a creative marriage.

Have Your Cake...

Cut two pieces of cake for each couple. Each couple must feed their spouse the cake, but they may not use any utensils, only fingers.

BRIDGE – Marriage is a give and take relationship. If what we give our spouse makes a mess, they will be tempted to retaliate. But, if we work together we can avoid many of the marriage messes.

Sign of the Times

Contact the members of your group before the meeting and ask them to bring their wedding pictures. Display the wedding pictures at your meeting. Let members of the group vote on different categories based on the wedding pictures. The following are examples of categories: couple that changed the most, couple that looks the same, best male hair style, best female hair style, etc.

BRIDGE – Marriages change over time. The way things were in the beginning are not always the way things are now. Marriage takes work. If we do not add to the work that got us to our wedding pictures we will not make it to anniversary pictures.

Wedding Music

Ask couples to try to remember the songs they had in their wedding. Compare the music that each couple used to see how many songs are similar. For added entertainment, let each couple choose which of their wedding songs was their favorite then try to sing the chorus.

BRIDGE – It is easy to forget many parts of the wedding day, but God wants us to remember our wedding day. That day is a significant day of covenant between God and your spouse. It takes work to remember and live out the important promises of our wedding days.

Wedding Dress Guess

Contact the wives prior to the meeting and ask them to bring their wedding dresses. Display the wedding dresses and let everyone try to guess which wedding dress matches each wife.

BRIDGE – We all change. Who we were on our wedding day may not be who we are now. The same is true with our relationships. It takes work to maintain a healthy relationship after the wedding.

HANDS-ON ACTIVITIES

Vow Redo

Let each couple rewrite their vows based on their experiences in marriage so far and what they expect in the coming years.

BRIDGE – It is hard to understand the depth of your vows on your wedding day. Your vows take on new meaning as you experience the rollercoaster ride of marriage.

Boys vs. Girls

Divide your group into males and females. Each group has to write new wedding vows. Once the vows are written, compare the two sets of vows and discuss the perspective of each gender as seen in the vows.

BRIDGE – Husbands and wives can have very different views on marriage. It takes working together to overcome the differences and build a healthy marriage.

General to Specific

There are parts of wedding vows that can be very general. Look through common wedding vows and discuss the specifics you have experienced from the general vows you took. For example: for better or worse, for richer or poorer, in sickness and in health, forsaking all others, etc.

BRIDGE – Even though we may not understand all the specifics of the vows we made, God still expects us to fulfill them. He gives us the strength to be faithful if we will trust in him as we learn the depth of the commitment we made to our spouse.

VISUAL REINFORCEMENTS

Wedding Pictures

Contact the members of your group before the meeting to ask them to bring their wedding pictures to be displayed at the meeting.

Wedding Reception

Put out food that reminds people of a wedding reception. Make hors d'oeuvres, wedding punch and a small cake.

MEDIA REINFORCEMENTS

"Canon in D" by Pachelbel

This is the traditional song played for the entrance of the bride. Ask the couples to try to remember their feelings on the day of their wedding when they heard this song. Remembering how we felt can be a powerful reminder of the commitment we made, but memories are not enough. It takes a current commitment to have a healthy marriage.

"Till Kingdom Come" by Coldplay

This song communicates one person's commitment to a relationship through all the events of life. Marriage takes a commitment that will not give up. It takes a commitment that will last no matter what obstacles come.

"White Flag" by Dido

The artist proclaims her undying commitment to love. The chorus tells that there will be no surrender, no raising the white flag on her love. God wants us to bring a no surrender approach to our marriage.

"I Walk the Line" by Johnny Cash

The promise in this song is to stay committed because of love. Walking the line means avoiding certain things that will damage your relationship as well as making choices to build the relationship.

"Follow Through" by Gavin DeGraw

He proclaims his love, but follows it up by saying if this relationship is going to work there must be follow through. The wedding day does not make the marriage. It takes follow through with a tireless MWE.

TAKE HOME OBJECT (Reminders of the lesson)

Written Statement

Print copies of Ed's modern day vernacular vows. Give each person a copy and have them sign and date it like they would a formal contract. Signing a contract can be intimidating because of its seriousness. There is something about seeing our name signed on an agreement that holds us accountable. We need to remember the significance of the commitment we made on our wedding day. By signing our vows we can use these papers as a reminder of the commitment we made.

Mirror Mirror...

Purchase small mirrors that can be passed out to each member of the group as a reminder to look in the mirror over the next few weeks of this study. This study is not about what your spouse can do to improve your marriage, it is about what you can do.

Tracking Your MWE

Print out calendars of the next month for each member of the group. Ask them to write down the work they put into their marriage. Then, use the calendars as a tool for making sure they are practicing a tireless MWE.

OTHER

Grapple Surprise

You can find grapples in your local grocery store. A grapple is an apple that tastes like a grape. Pass out samples of grapples without telling the members of your group what they are.

BRIDGE – Marriage is not always what we expect. There are times we discover what marriage really is only after we have made the commitment and experience it.

Best Decisions

Let couples share what they believe are some of the best decisions they made for the health of their marriage.

BRIDGE – Great marriages do not just happen. They take conscious decisions that are accompanied by tireless work.

Wedding Day Disasters

Let couples share some of the events that seemed like disasters on the day of their wedding.

BRIDGE – Successful marriages do not give up. Remember the tenacity that you used to overcome those wedding day disasters and apply it to current obstacles.

Write God a thank you note for giving you that blessing.

CREATIVE COMMUNICATION

LEADER'S NOTES

1. Pick three words to describe communication with your spouse before you got married.

Tip: One way to increase the communication between spouses in this session is to let the spouses work together for a few minutes to pick out the words that describe their communication before they got married. Then, let the spouses share their three words and explain why they chose them.

3. What are examples of "spoiled fish" comments you made while communicating with your spouse?

It is easy to use a "spoiled fish" comment when the heat is on in an argument. The comments turn from constructive to destructive. Instead of bringing up issues for discussion issues are brought up for the destruction of your spouse. This type of attacking comments leaves a foul smell lingering with your spouse.

Tip: Don't forget that this is a time to share your own comments and not the comments your spouse made. If it turns into a time to "tattle" on your spouse, this question will do more damage than good.

3. How do "spoiled fish" comments affect your desire to communicate with your spouse?

"Spoiled fish" comments make you want to shut down the lines of true communication. When someone lobs these destructive comments into the conversation, they escalate emotions which can prevent listening and understanding the other person's side. And, if there is any response to a "spoiled fish" comment it is generally more retaliatory than constructive.

The result of "spoiled fish" comments can be disastrous

during the conversation as well as constricting in the future. The next time there is the need to discuss an issue; you will be hesitant to bring it up if you know there is a good chance you are going to get hit with destructive comments. Those issues that are not discussed fester and the lines of communication further deteriorate.

4. What are some ways your spouse has built you up with encouraging comments?

Tip: Encourage as many people as possible to share. For some couples, it will be hard to admit there are encouraging comments because the communication lines are so battered, but it is important for everyone to acknowledge something encouraging their spouse has done. By giving this positive recognition it can open up future lines of communication for encouraging comments.

5. What are other ways you could take an "e-Break" with your spouse?

Phone calls, text messages and instant emails via a Blackberry (or whatever you use) can extinguish any hopes of communication with your spouse. When you go on a date, leave the electronics at home. Or, if you want a phone so the babysitter can get a hold of you in an emergency, take the phone that is least likely to get a phone call and only answer the babysitter's call.

6. Tell a time you had poor results from trying to communicate with your spouse in the wrong zone.

Tip: Start by identifying each person's zone. You can do this by finding out what part of the day they are the most productive. Then, once you know each person's zone, reverse it to find out the wrong zone.

7. Brainstorm a list of recreational activities couples could do together to help communication.

The key to these activities is interaction. Activities that involve large groups of people might spur communication, but not necessarily with your spouse. If you are going to participate in something that has a lot of other people involved, find a way for you to be partnered with your spouse. Also, look for activities that remove distractions. If you choose an activity that adds stress and tension, that could have a diminishing effect on your communication.

10. What have you done to overcome the obstacles that come with a date night?

Tip: One of the most difficult obstacles of date nights can be finding childcare. If that seems to be a common concern in your group, encourage the couples to start a childcare co-op. For example, partner with a couple and set one night of the week to be a date night. Then, rotate which couple goes on the date and which couple keeps the kids. This is a way to get a date night with free childcare twice a month.

11. Brainstorm two lists of options for date nights. Make one list consisting of inexpensive ideas that stay under $20. Then, make a second list of other options for date nights that will cost more.

Tip: Write down all the ideas then email your group the ideas later in the week. This will provide a resource for couples as they try to make plans for future dates.

10. When is the best time for you to have a sweet sixteen?

Think back to the section on playing in the right zone. Remember when you and your spouse are most effective and when you are in the wrong zone. Then, think about the schedule of your home. When you first get home might be one of the most chaotic times of your day. If that is the case, have your sweet sixteen when things settle down. Remember, the goal of the sweet sixteen is not to check it off your list. The goal is intimate communication so pick a time that is right for the goal.

11. What are some reason-free gifts you would like to receive?

Tip: Once again, write down these ideas and email them to your group along with the date night ideas. If you do this, by the end of the lesson your group should have a great list of practical ideas for improving communication in their marriage.

CREATIVE NOTES

ICEBREAKERS

Love Letters

Contact members before the meeting and ask them to bring old love letters from before they were married or in the early years of their marriage. Take turns reading and showing these relationship artifacts.

BRIDGE – Communication is an important part of marriage. While communication seems to come easier in the early stages of the relationship, it is just as important in the later stages. It takes work to build creative communication.

Newly Wed Game

The newly wed game attempts to see how well spouses know each other. There are two rounds. In the first round, the ladies leave the room and the guys are asked a series of questions while writing down their answers. The ladies are asked to answer the same questions based on what they think their husband would answer while writing down their answers. Then, the couples are reunited and answers are compared. For the second round, the same thing happens except this time the men leave the room and the questions are answered from the wife's perspective. Each couple is awarded points for matching answers and the couple with the most points at the end of the game wins.

The following are some sample questions for the game:

- Where was your first date?
- What was the last movie you saw together in the theater?
- What is your favorite restaurant?
- What is your favorite TV show?
- What is the brand of laundry detergent used in your house?
- What do you like on your hamburger?
- When was the last date you went on?
- When was the last time you said "I love you"?

BRIDGE – It takes a lot of communication to know your spouse. If you want to keep communication fresh you have to find creative ways to keep the conversations going.

What Did You Say?

While English is the official language of the United States, it sounds differently depending on what part of America you live in. There are words, phrases and expressions used that are isolated to certain regions. For example, if you are offering someone a soft drink in the south you might ask them, "Would you like a Coke®?" even if you are offering Dr. Pepper® or Pepsi®. What are other examples of jargon that is unique to different parts of the country?

BRIDGE – We all bring unique parts of our communication into marriage. It takes time to learn how your spouse communicates and to learn how to communicate with them.

HANDS-ON ACTIVITIES

In the Bucket

Set a bucket on the ground then have a member of your group stand about 5 feet from the bucket with their back to the bucket. Give them small balls to try to throw in the bucket without looking at the bucket. Let them try 3 to 5 times without any help. Then, let them try again except this time the rest of the group can help by telling them how to adjust the next throw.

BRIDGE – Communication is essential if you want to hit your target. It takes giving your spouse permission to help you correct issues and taking the advice when it is given to you.

One at a Time

Give one couple two different magazine or newspaper articles. Tell each spouse to pick a paragraph then read it out loud to each other at the same time. Once they are done reading, have them try to describe what their spouse just read.

BRIDGE – Communication is better when it is done one person at a time. If we talk over our spouse and think about what we are going to say instead of listening we will miss out on true communication.

Just Because

Homemade cards can be some of the most memorable. Offer construction paper, scissors, markers and pens to make homemade cards for their spouses. Give everyone time during the meeting to be creative and make a card that communicates what they feel about their spouse.

BRIDGE – "Just because" gifts will only happen when you take time to make them happen. They are a great way to communicate your love to your spouse in a creative manner.

VISUAL REINFORCEMENTS

Obey the Signs

Make signs with each of the communication suggestions from this chapter. For example, for "Take an e-Break" make a sign with a cell phone crossed out; for "Observe Speed-Limit Signs" make speed limit signs; etc.

MEDIA REINFORCEMENTS

"Voices Carry" by 'Til Tuesday

This 80's classic describes a couple with communication problems. The girl can't figure out what the guy is thinking and when she tries to talk with him the only response she gets is "Hush Hush. Keep it down now. Voices carry." Not being willing to listen can be a communication killer.

"From Me to You" by the Beatles

In this song, one person is encouraged to tell the other if there is anything they can say or do for the other person. We need this type of receptive attitude to the needs our spouse communicates.

"I Wanna Talk About Me" by Toby Keith

This song is written from a guy's point of view that is tired of just talking about his girlfriend and wants to talk about him as well. There are times we need to be as blunt as this song and talk about what we want and need.

"Words of Love" by The Mamas and the Papas

This song is a warning that the same old words of love will not work forever. There has to be creativity in the communication.

"These Words" by Natasha Bedingfield

A writer struggles for the right words to communicate her feelings but cannot come up with anything better than I love you. We cannot neglect the importance of telling our spouse, "I love you."

TAKE HOME OBJECT (Reminders of the lesson)

Post-It

Pass out pads of sticky notes and encourage the members to write little love notes to their spouse and post them around the house.

Write it Down

Pass out index cards and let members write down what they love about their spouse. Then, have them give the cards to their spouses.

Communication Vows

Make copies of the following communication vows and pass them out to the members of your group:
- I commit to regularly take e-breaks, play in the right zone, observe the speed-limit signs, pursue recreational companionship, do the math, enjoy the sweet sixteen and give gifts just because.

Speeding Tickets

Design and print fake speeding tickets to give to the members of the group. Encourage them to give these speeding tickets to their spouse when schedules start getting too busy.

Reading the Signs

In our busy lives, we can use help reading our spouses signs. Pass out index cards that are green, yellow and red. Place these cards on your refrigerator or some other prominent position. When communication is going good, leave the green card on top. When problems are starting to occur, put the yellow card on top. When there is a problem, put the red card on top. Use the colors to help you stay in tune with your spouse and make time to discuss what is wrong anytime there is anything less than green.

OTHER

Conversation Piece

Sometimes starting an interesting conversation can be the most difficult part. There are books designed to help spark communication. Try ideas from the books "Conversation Piece" and "Conversation Piece 2" by Bret Nicholaus and Paul Lowrie to start communication.

BRIDGE – Communication takes work. Don't be afraid to use whatever resources are available to inspire creative communication.

Work In vs. Work On

Doing work in your marriage and doing work on your marriage are two different things. Running errands, doing the budget and cleaning the house are all examples of work we do "in" our marriages. Taking assessments of the health of your marriage and going on date nights are examples of working "on" our marriage. What are other examples of things you can do to work "on" your marriage?

BRIDGE – Creative communication is a key to making sure you are not just doing work in your marriage, but that you are working on your marriage.

CREATIVE CONFLICT

CREATIVE MARRIAGE

LEADER'S NOTES

1. **How do you handle conflict? Read through the following scenarios and discuss how you would handle each one.**
   - You are standing in the "10 items or less" line at the grocery store when you notice the person in front of you has at least 15 items.
   - You notice a car pulling out of a parking space in a crowded parking lot. You put your turn signal on and wait for the car to move. Once the car has pulled out of the space, someone cuts in front of you and takes the parking spot.
   - You are talking with a group of friends when one of them makes an offensive comment about you. You know the friend did not mean to be offensive with the comment, but it was.

   Tip: Try to have fun with these scenarios. Encourage everyone to participate so you can get a variety of responses. Once you have gone through the answers, encourage each person to think about their answers and what they can learn about their conflict style from those answers. Are they the type of person who rushes to conflict? Do they avoid conflict at all costs? Are they loud and irrational or do they calmly reason their way to a solution?

2. **Fights happen in marriage, and not always for good reasons. What are bad reasons you have fought with your spouse?**

   One bad reason to fight with your spouse is that you are taking out your anger on them from another issue. When other problems get drug into the marriage, it can cause conflict that would have previously been ignored. Selfishness can be another bad reason to fight. Sometimes you can put the spotlight on yourself and it blinds you to the needs of those around you.

3. Evaluate yourself. In a fight are you frequently tempted to launch verbal missiles? If so, what could you do to help control the urge?

It may sound a bit cheesy, but taking deep breaths and counting to ten before responding can be a great way to diffuse potential verbal missiles. Keeping a respectful tone throughout the conflict can also help. When the situation gets too intense, it is easier to launch verbal missiles without thinking about it. Also, think about your spouse. Before you say what is on your mind, take time to think about how it will affect your spouse. Finally, say a quick prayer when you feel a conflict brewing. Ask God to control your tongue and help you model the character of Christ throughout your conflict.

6. What are some examples of "gentle answers" you could use in a conflict?

Harsh words can look different depending on the couple. For one couple, anything said in a raised tone is considered harsh. For others, harsh words don't enter the picture until there are screams and personal attacks. Talk with your spouse about what they consider a harsh word. If you don't, you might think you are using gentle answers but it will not come across that way to your spouse.

7. Why do you think it is tempting to drag up the past or other issues in arguments?

When you corner a wild animal, they can do incredible things to fight their way out. They will use unprecedented force and violence to find a way out. This same instinct can arise in couples during a conflict. When one spouse feels attacked by another they might do anything they can think of to find a way out. If that means digging back into the past to find something to fight their way out with, they will use it.

Dragging up past issues or other issues can also be a sign of unresolved conflict. If the previous issue was never resolved, it can come rushing into your mind once the conflict starts. The result is all the emotions of the unresolved conflict gets drug into the current conflict.

6. What could you do to help you put the conflict behind you when it is over?

Don't take the easy way out. When you are dealing with a conflict, work until the answer is found. It can be tempting to find a quick fix for the conflict, but this can result in only putting a bandage on the problem instead of resolving it. If you want to put a conflict behind you, there must be a resolution that both sides can accept. Do the work and find that answer.

7. What could you do to help you fight the temptation to focus on your spouse's speck while ignoring your own Sequoia?

Instead of going into attack mode, go into resolve mode. The difference is that in attack mode, you are on the offensive and focused on your target. You are in a self-preservation mindset as well and the result can be ignoring your own Sequoia. When you go into resolve mode, you take a step back to see the big picture. You take the time to look at the conflict from different angles. This helps you clearly identify the specks in your spouse's eye while noticing the Sequoia in your own eye.

8. What have you done that helps you listen more attentively?

Slowing down the pace of the conversation can help in listening. This allows you to listen to what your spouse is saying without having to formulate your answer at the same time. When the pace of the conversation is slower you can listen to your spouse, ask questions about what they are saying and make sure you understand them before you start to form your response.

9. Think about the following issues then tell what a pre you-turn statement might be then what a statement after a you-turn might sound like.
   • **Your spouse is spending too much money**

   "You are blowing our budget! You are making us go broke!" vs. "I feel like you are not sticking to the budget."
   • **Your spouse is not helping you do work around the house**

   "You never do anything around here!" vs. "I need more help around the house."
   • **The amount of intimacy in your relationship is lacking**

   "You never want to have sex!" vs. "I do not feel like we are having sex enough."

10. Why do you think using the D-word can be dangerous in a marriage?

Divorce is the last act in a relationship. By using the D-word you are jumping over all the opportunities for resolution and going straight to the termination. Also, divorce is giving up on the relationship so to use the D-word is a threat to give up on the relationship. If you are threatening to give up, that should scare your spouse away from putting effort into the relationship. In the end, using the D-word can be a self-fulfilling prophecy.

11. Describe how God has helped you work through issues in the past.

Tip: Come to the meeting with some creative ways you have worked through issues in the past. As others answer, try to find what each couple did that could be applied to other couples in general. Also, emphasize how many options there are in a conflict. This may encourage those who feel like they are in a conflict without any options.

CREATIVE NOTES

ICEBREAKERS

Where'd That Come From?

Have you ever examined what you do in a conflict? Think about your most common reactions in conflict. Then, think about the way your parents handled conflict. How much of your parents' conflict style is a part of your conflict style?

BRIDGE – Just because you learned to handle conflict one way does not mean that is the right way. Even if your parents taught you great techniques for handling conflict, you can still be creative and find even better ways to overcome conflicts.

Old News

Drag out several of your yearbooks. Show embarrassing pictures of when you were in high school and middle school. Ask the group about embarrassing fashion trends they were into during high school?

BRIDGE – It is one thing when we bring up mistakes of our past, but nobody likes it when others drag them up. When you are in a conflict, stick with the present issue and don't drag up past issues.

HANDS-ON ACTIVITIES

Shake It Up

Pass out small bottles of a soft drink to several members of your group. Have them shake up those bottles for 30 seconds. Then, the contest is to see who can take the cap off the quickest without spilling any of the drink.

BRIDGE – We all know how to carefully handle a volatile soft drink. Yet, when it comes to handling a volatile situation with our spouse we sometimes are more careful with a soft drink than them. Handling conflict takes care and creativity.

Natural Disaster Damage

Print off pictures of the damage from natural disasters and pass them around for the members of the group to see.

BRIDGE – When we do not work at conflict it can be a natural disaster that leads to horrific damage in our relationships.

Chipping In

For this activity, you will need to be outside. Get a bucket, a pitching wedge and wiffle golf balls. Take turns trying to get the wiffle golf balls into the bucket using the pitching wedge.

BRIDGE – Hitting the ball is the easy part. Getting the ball to go where you want is the challenge. Fighting it out in a conflict is easy. Getting the conflict to move in a healthy direction is the difficult part. It takes creativity to bring progress out of conflict.

VISUAL REINFORCEMENTS

Boxing Gloves

Put out boxing gloves or other fight gear as a visual reminder for the way many of us handle conflict.

Dart Board

Put out a dart board and darts where everyone can see it. Use this as a reminder of the danger of throwing verbal darts in a conflict.

MEDIA REINFORCEMENTS

"We Can Work it Out" by the Beatles

The song is a request for another person to see a situation from a new perspective. The artist wants the other person to "try to see it my way." If we are going to overcome conflict, we have to try to see the issue from both perspectives.

"My Confession" by Josh Groban

The artist admits that he has been wrong about the other person. He confesses his wrongdoing and admits his true feelings. Communication is a large part of creatively resolving conflict.

"Dedicated to the One I Love" by The Mamas and the Papas

The song is a request for the other person in the relationship to whisper a prayer for the other person, every night before bed. When you pray together before you go to sleep it will help you apply the principle of not letting the sun go down on your anger.

"Always on my Mind" by Willie Nelson

He apologizes for not communicating his love the way he should have. Sometimes, we just need to admit we were wrong and apologize.

"The Good Stuff" by Kenny Chesney

The character in this song hides out in a bar after a fight with his spouse. The character orders the "good stuff" and the bartender tells him the "good stuff" comes from working out your problems at home. We may be tempted to run from our problems, but the best solution is to stay and work them out.

Rocky

Show clips from the final fight scenes in any of the Rocky movies. Just like Rocky, we can overcome the odds and win our conflicts.

TAKE HOME OBJECT (Reminders of the lesson)

Wave the Flag

Pass out small pieces of cloth to remind us to wave the flag of good manners.

OTHER

Dead Right

A father told his son, "you can be right, but you can be dead right too." There are times you might be right, but demanding that your right way is accepted by others can cost you too much. There are times in a conflict when exerting that you are right is not worth it. What are some examples of time you might be right in a conflict but it is better to give in to the other person?

BRIDGE – There is a time to stand up when you are right, and a time to defer to the other person. If you always have to be right in a conflict, you will only make some conflicts worse.

Gentle Answer

Write down a list of things that commonly generate conflict. For example, who takes off work if a child is sick, budget issues, etc. Then, read Proverbs 15:1. Discuss gentle answers in the conflicts that could help, and what are harsh words that will make the conflict worse.

BRIDGE – Conflicts will arise. We must choose to use gentle answers in conflict if we do not want to create further problems.

CREATIVE INTIMACY

CREATIVE MARRIAGE

LEADER'S NOTES

1. Explain what voices you think are the most influential when it comes to sex.

One of the most influential voices about sex is advertising. Their influence comes from the sheer volume of sex related advertisements. There are billboards, print ads, commercials and a host of new ideas every day for a product to get noticed. Many of these products choose sexual content as the focus of their advertisements. That is an influential factor.

Hollywood churns out songs, television shows and movies with messages on sex ranging from blatant to near subliminal. They set certain expectations and influence already formed ideas. They are intentional in the ideas they communicate about sex.

Another influencer when it comes to sex is peer relationships. The conversations you have with friends influence what you think is normal. The conversations you overhear in the office or other public places can be just as influential.

The church is also a voice in the conversation about sex. The influence of the church in the sexual arena has been under attack, but it is still a voice. Along with the church comes the family. Many of the most basic ideas about sex start in the home.

2. Do you think most people outside the church believe God is pro-sex? Explain your answer.

The message that is commonly spread in the media is that God is against sex. In movies and television, the Christian characters are commonly boycotting anything related to sex. Newscasts cover teenagers who commit to stay pure until marriage. The angle on this story is commonly that "students give up sex" or something like that that sounds as if those who follow God are against sex.

God is not against sex. God created sex. If he did not want sex to happen he would have created another way for procreation. God is against sex apart from his plan. God designed sex to have healthy parameters and when those parameters are broken, sex can have consequences. The message of "Sex God's Way" has been translated into "No Sex" but that is not accurate.

3. Why do you think the church has historically avoided teaching about sex in a positive way?

Some teachers in the church have relied on scare tactics to influence their congregation. Instead of painting the whole picture that God paints on issues, it can be easier to just talk about the punishments. The result is the consequences of sex have sometimes been emphasized without discussing the positives.

Also, well meaning church members have lumped all discussions about sex into one "sinful" category. In an effort to encourage purity, sex has been ignored instead of being taught based on God's principles. But, God intended for the church and the family to talk about sex and teach how to enjoy sex in a pure and God honoring way.

4. How does this biblical principle about sexuality differ from what is commonly believed?

The message sent from an early age in our society is that your body is your own. The Bible busts that idea. When a couple gets married, the two become one and each person has a right to the other just as each person has a right to their own body.

Also, this principle teaches that sexual fulfillment is an obligation in the marriage. Most couples think finding a way to sexually satisfy their spouse is an option, but not based on God. He knows the importance of a healthy sexual relationship in marriage so he emphasizes the responsibility.

5. Brainstorm a list of words you think describes the opposite gender's sex drive.

Tip: There are no right or wrong answers for this question. Let everyone know they are free to share their opinions without having to worry about being wrong. Ask for explanations of the words that were chosen. Also, keep control of the conversation so that it does not get out of hand leading to something being said that will later be regretted.

6. How have you commonly seen sex portrayed through popular media?

Some popular media commonly portrays sex as consequence free. "There is no right or wrong way as long as you follow your heart." This carefree attitude promotes promiscuity and infidelity.

There is another group of popular media that has recently been pushing responsible sex. This is a "safe sex" movement advocating resources to prevent the spread of sexually transmitted diseases.

7. What could you start this week to take better care of your temple?

Tip: Let your group know it does not have to be an "all or nothing" decision. They do not have to go from eating fast food everyday and wearing a rut in their couch to running marathons. The transformation does not have to be a complete shift from dressing like a high school student to "GQ" or "Vogue" magazine. Taking better care of your temple can be as simple as cutting out soft drinks, cutting down on dessert or letting your spouse clean out your closet.

8. What are some of the most common excuses for a married couple not having sex, and what percentage of those excuses do you think are legitimate?

There are legitimate excuses for not having sex. But, those excuses are only temporarily legitimate. If you commonly have the excuse that you are too tired, you need to examine what is making you so tired and find a way to fix it. If you are struggling to overcome emotional scars, work to identify them and move on. Legitimate answers turn illegitimate when nothing is done to fix them.

9. What are some reasonably inexpensive retreats you have taken, or heard that others have taken?

Tip: Use your room full of minds to help you create inexpensive retreats. Think creatively and discover how you can make the most of the resources you have instead of limiting yourself with what you do not have.

10. What are common areas in a marriage where monotony can set in?

Monotony can strike every area of marriage. If you are not proactive, you will find yourself having the same fights, then making up the same way, having the same conversations, the same dates, the same romantic retreats and the same problems. It takes a commitment to creativity to keep from falling prey to monotony.

11. Men, tell the women some scenarios that you think are romantic.

Tip: For questions 11 and 12, you might want to let the husbands work together and the wives work together for a few minutes so they have less pressure to come up with romantic ideas on their own. This will also encourage more people to share since they are working as a team to come up with ideas instead of just relying on their own ideas.

12. Women, tell the men some scenarios that you think are romantic.

CREATIVE NOTES

ICEBREAKERS:

Home Schooling

What comes to your mind when you hear the term, "The Talk"? The first talk with your parents about sex can have a lasting impression. Describe what happened when you received "the talk" with your parents. Was it strictly scientific? Were there moments of memorable advice?

BRIDGE – Most of us have heard talks about the scientific side of sexual intimacy, but there is much more than the scientific side. Creative intimacy is knowing more than just the scientific.

Word Association

Brainstorm a list of words that describe the female and the male sex drive. Then, compare the two and describe why you think God designed males and females that way.

BRIDGE – True intimacy comes from a partnership despite our differences. When we learn to work together, God can use our unique design to enhance the intimacy instead of tearing it down.

Good Intentions

Sometimes the most romantic moments can come from what should have been a romantic flop. In those moments of romantic failure, it can really be the thought that counts. What are examples of romantic ideas gone wrong in your relationship?

BRIDGE – Not every romantic idea works out. To keep the intimacy creative, it takes a commitment to press on past the failures.

HANDS-ON ACTIVITIES

Your Best and Worst List

Pass out entertainment or fashion magazines and make up your own best dressed and worst dressed list. Let everyone pick out people from the magazines they want to nominate for the best and worst dressed. Then, as a group, vote on your best and worst dressed male as well as the best and worst dressed female.

Don't give up on fashion and hygiene when you get married. Think about personal hygiene and fashion, but not just for your own sake. Find out what your spouse likes and try to be on their best dressed list.

Telephone Game

Play the telephone game. Whisper a message to the person beside you then have them whisper what they heard to the person next to them. Keep this up until the message has been passed around the group. Then, let the last person tell what they heard.

BRIDGE – In the telephone game, the message always gets messed up. This is the danger of sharing sacred stuff from your marriage. The message will get spread around and inevitably end up messed up. Sacred stuff needs to stay in the confines of your marriage.

Hallmark Moment

Break into groups of 3 to 4 and pass out materials to make the ultimate valentine card. Have each team make what they consider the ultimate valentine card then share it with the other groups.

BRIDGE – Creative intimacy does not have to be expensive. You can experience romantic moments for virtually no expense if you will work at it and make a commitment to keep it creative. This means moving out of your comfort zone and taking intimacy risks.

VISUAL REINFORCEMENT

Superglue

Spread out tubes of superglue and pieces of Velcro®. Sex apart from God's principles creates a Velcro bond. Sex done God's way creates a superglue bond in the marriage.

Act It Out

Instead of just telling the example under "Sex Builder #2" from Dr. Willard Harley, act it out for the group to see the effects of not dialing into your spouse's sex drive.

Romantic Getaways

Contact members of your group and ask them to bring pictures from their favorite romantic getaways. Show the pictures and share about the experiences.

MEDIA REINFORCEMENTS

"Ring of Fire" by Johnny Cash

In this song, the singer fell into the red hot flames of passion. Those flames are enticing in the beginning, but if we do not work at intimacy the ring of fire we fell into will go out.

"You Got to Me" by Neil Diamond

The artist found a girl that got to him in a good way. Creative intimacy is about finding out what "gets to your spouse" in a good way and doing that.

"Tell Her About It" by Billy Joel

The artist is warning another man to not make the same mistake he did. The advice is to communicate his feelings, wants and desires to the woman he loves. In creative intimacy, we must make communicating our wants and desires a priority to our spouse.

"I Want You, I Need You, I Love You" by Elvis Presley

The artist confesses his feelings. One key line is, "I thought I could live without romance, until you came to me." We need to think about our favorite aspects of our spouse and let that bring out the romance in us.

TAKE HOME OBJECT

Superglue

Pass out tubes of superglue as a reminder that God wants to use creative intimacy as a tool to superglue the bond of marriage.

OTHER

Most Romantic Scenes

Brainstorm romantic movies then vote for what you think are the top 3 romantic movies. Or, let the guys vote for what they think are the most romantic movies and let the girls vote for what they think are the most romantic movies. Compare what guys consider romantic and what girls consider romantic.

BRIDGE – God has wired men and women differently, especially when it comes to romance. The key is to communicate with your spouse what you think is romantic and make efforts to be romantic for each other.

Books-A-Million

Suggest books that are good for intimacy from a Christian perspective like "The Gift of Sex: A Guide to Sexual Fulfillment" by Drs. Cliff and Joyce Penner, "Sheet Music" Dr. Kevin Leman, "Sex Begins in the Kitchen" by Kevin Leman, "Sex 101" by Clifford and Joyce Penner, "Celebration of Sex After 50" by Dr. Douglas E. Rosenau and Dr. Jim and Carolyn Childerston.

BRIDGE – Keeping intimacy creative sometimes means going beyond what we know about the subject and learning from others.

CREATIVE FINANCES

CREATIVE MARRIAGE

LEADER'S NOTES

1. Describe the worst bite or sting you have received.

2. Think back to your early credit card days. How old were you when you first got a credit card and how well did you use your credit card?

Tip: Let people in your group share how they got their first credit card. Find out if they were solicited or if they looked for it on their own. How hard was it to get a credit card? What were some of their first credit card purchases?

3. Do a wallet check now. How many credit cards do you have in your wallet?

Tip: Do not make it embarrassing to admit how many credit cards they have. Having a bunch of credit cards does not make you a bad manager of your finances if you use them wisely.

4. How can debt make you feel enslaved?

Debt can make you feel like a slave by taking away your freedom. The constant calls from creditors take up your time. The fear of losing what you have keeps you from enjoying it. The strain of trying to catch up on payments can make you unable to appreciate the other areas of your life. And if you do not make payments on what you owe, you could lose everything you have. It is almost as if your debtor owns all your stuff until you finishing making payments.

5. Why do you think God describes those who do not repay what they borrow as "wicked"?

If you borrow but do not repay, you are essentially stealing. You have taken something that does not belong to you and not paid for it. It also calls your honesty into question because you made a commitment to pay back what you owed, but did not do it.

6. How does God's view of debt differ from what is communicated by society as a whole?

Society encourages you to borrow as much as you want and not think about the consequences. God wants you to borrow only when you know you can repay. Society encourages you to be frivolous with other people's money. God desires you to be careful with money regardless of whose it is.

7. Who do you think has some of the most effective advertisements?

Tip: Pull advertisements from magazines or newspapers as examples. You could also show commercials you have recorded. Another way to show the effectiveness of some advertisements is to let your group come up with product jingles or slogans letting the rest of the group try to guess what product they are connected to. This would emphasize the effectiveness of many advertisements.

8. How could you be wise when you see tempting advertisements?

Advertisements show you a limited view. If you want to be wise when you look at advertisements, back away and try to see the big picture. Think about the cost to gain what is advertised. Compare what else you could have if you did not give in to the advertisements. The biggest part of being wise is taking time to look at all the sides of the product and not just the side that is being advertised.

9. Describe a time you did something you would not have done without peer pressure.

Peer pressure is alive long beyond graduation. As an adult it is commonly referred to as "keeping up with the Joneses." Your neighbor gets a new car so you feel pressured to upgrade. Your friends take a fancy vacation so you feel the need to take a vacation. The pressure can be daunting.

However, peer pressure does not have to be a negative influence. If you have positive relationships, your peer pressure can influence you to be more faithful with your money.

10. If you tithe, how has it positively affected your life?

Tip: Contact couples in your group that you know tithe and ask them to come ready to share their experiences with tithing.

11. What are some of the common reasons given for not saving more?

The needs versus wants trap can be a big player in not saving. The media and other influences try to make their products seem like a necessity. In reality, they are just something you want. So, money that could be going to savings is spent other places. For example, cable television or satellite television is not a necessity. Those are wants that can begin to seem like needs.

12. **What are some strategies that could help you either start saving or start saving more?**

    Write down what you spend and make sure you know where every dollar goes. You might find that you are carelessly spending money that could be saved. Learn to delay your gratification. Instead of buying a product as soon as you want it, delay the purchase and save your money. You may find out you did not want that purchase as much as you originally thought. Also, start saving something. It does not have to be 10% right off the bat. Start saving whatever you can and work your way up.

13. **How do you think applying the give, give, live principle could help you enjoy the money you spend?**

    When you can have whatever you want, it can diminish your appreciation of the things you have. By working and saving for a purchase, it can make you appreciate it all the more. Also, if you are living by God's principles for your finances, you can enjoy the things you have guilt free because you know you are honoring God with your money.

CREATIVE NOTES

ICEBREAKERS:

Coolest Card Contest

Compare credit cards to see who has the coolest looking credit card.

BRIDGE – Credit card companies do everything they can to make their cards as appealing as possible. It is up to us to see through the surface level attractions and find out the real deal with the credit cards we own.

Neighbor See, Neighbor Do

Keeping up with the Joneses can be very evident in neighborhoods. One home does new landscaping, then before you know it there are many homes with similar landscaping. One home gets a new toy like a hot tub, pool, basketball goal, and before you know it there are many new toys in the neighborhood. How have you seen neighbor see, neighbor do in your neighborhood?

BRIDGE – The pressure to stay up with the spending pace of our neighbors can be enormous. The key is to implement biblical principles that help control our spending.

Are the Best Things in Life Free?

Brainstorm a list of what you consider the best things in life and determine if money is a factor in obtaining the best things in life.

BRIDGE – Money is not a bad thing. Money can be a part of helping us enjoy some of the best things in life. The key is to not let money become one of your favorite things in life.

HANDS-ON ACTIVITIES

Needs vs. Wants

On a large sheet of paper, make two columns. In one column write "Needs" and in the other column write "Wants". Brainstorm typical expenses and discuss if they are a reasonable need or a want. By reasonable, take into consideration where you live. For example, a car is not a need in a 3rd world tribe, but one car might be a reasonable need in your community.

BRIDGE – It can be hard to distinguish between some needs and wants. Media plays a big part in convincing us that we need things that are really just wants. We have to be cautious not to buy into the media hype.

Favorite Commercials

Divide into groups of three to four and brainstorm the most memorable commercials. Then, let each group act out their favorite commercial while the other groups try to guess.

BRIDGE – Commercials are designed to stick with us. The companies want their advertisements to stay in our minds and influence us. We have to be careful to not let the commercials control us.

They're Everywhere

Pass out magazines or newspapers to search for advertisements that overemphasize the good and put the warnings in less prominent places. Show the ads that hide the cautions and discuss how that is the common theme of commercials (to overemphasize the good and downplay the cautions).

BRIDGE – Advertisers are finding new ways to advertise and new places to display their ads all the time. But, one thing that remains constant is advertisers' ability to emphasize the good and hide the bad. We must look beyond the good that is being emphasized and look at both sides of the product.

VISUAL REINFORCEMENT

Endless Offers

Save the credit card offers you get in your mail between meetings. Spread them out in front of your group and show how many offers you got in that short period of time. You could read the offers trying to find the most enticing.

Cutting the Credit Out

Put a large pair of scissors in the middle of your group as a visual reminder that at times we need to take drastic action to eliminate our credit card problems.

MEDIA REINFORCEMENTS

Commercials

Record commercials then show them during your meeting. After watching each commercial, try to decipher what the advertisement is selling in addition to the product. For example, the beer commercial that sells sex.

"Money (That's What I Want)" by the Beatles

The premise of this song is that there are great things that are free, but they don't compare to what money can get. This is the mindset of many people. Examine your spending habits to see if you have bought into this song's mindset.

"Luckenbach, Texas (Back to the Basics of Love)" by Waylon Jennings

The artist becomes tired of trying to keep up with the Joneses. The pressure to live a high society life becomes too much so he wants to move to a slower place and live a simple life. We can get caught up in the rat race and miss out on the pleasure of living a simple life.

TAKE HOME OBJECT

10-10-80

Make cards for wallets and checkbooks that say 10-10-80 as a reminder.

OTHER

Credit Card-iac Arrest

Describe a time you got a credit card bill significantly higher than expected. How did you react and did you make changes or did the high bills continue?

BRIDGE – Credit card debt can easily catch us off guard and the results can be shocking. God has a plan for us to avoid credit card-iac arrest.

Spending Habits

Think about your spending habits over the past few months. What were the items that blew your budget? Or, if you stayed on your budget, what are the most tempting items for you to blow your budget?

BRIDGE – Everyone has areas of temptation to blow the budget. If you notice that you consistently overspend in one area of your budget, it might be that instead of cutting out that expense, you need to redo your budget. A budget is only effective when it also takes into account how you want to enjoy your money.

CREATIVE PRIORITIES

CREATIVE MARRIAGE

LEADER'S NOTES

1. Do you think some people are just wired to be a good spouse or a good parent if not both?

Sometimes it can feel like some people have an extra spouse or parenting gene that others do not. Those people make being a spouse or being a parent seem so effortless. They seem to always know what to do and what to say. While there are probably some characteristics that make being a good spouse or parent easier, it is not likely that anybody is just wired to be a good spouse or parent. Everybody has to work at it if they want to be good.

2. Explain whether or not you think it is easier to be a good spouse or a good parent.

For some, the parenting gig comes easier while for others being a spouse seems to be easier. Some people are naturally nurturers, so for them parenting might be right up their alley while that same nurturing side could drive their spouse crazy. Or, somebody could find compromise and partnership easy which could be great with their spouse, but too much compromising and partnership could spoil a child. Both are difficult and your personality could play into which one you think is easier.

3. Do you think the average parent today is better, the same or worse than parents in the 1950's? Take time to explain your opinion.

Tip: Take into consideration the cultural climate of the 1950's. Children might have been more obedient, but was that because the parents were better? Or was it because there were fewer influences encouraging kids to disobey? Parents today have more access to material showing them how their kids think and develop, but does that really help based on what you see?

4. What do you think the average parent would say if you asked them for a definition of parenting?

There might be different definitions of parenting for every person you ask. Some think parenting is about being a friend. Others think parenting is about instilling discipline at whatever cost. Some might even think parenting is just about getting through it so it is meaningless to try to define it.

5. What do you think keeps so many parents from putting the marriage at the top of the family food chain?

Children have a strange way of demanding attention. Their needs are more apparent. Their desires are made known more readily. Parents also get pleasure from giving to their children. The gifts could be tangible like toys or intangible like time and attention. Add to this the strong and instantaneous love parents feel for their children and it is not hard to understand how the children can move to the top of the family food chain. Meanwhile, the spouse does not demand attention. They do not put their needs out there like a child. The result is the spouse is easily neglected.

6. What are other ways you can put attention for your spouse at the top of the priority list in your home?

The main thing is to carve out time specifically set aside to give your spouse attention. Do not let it be invaded with other activities, people or any other distractions. Also, find out what type of attention your spouse likes. They may like intimate conversations, sharing activities or acts of service. Whatever type of attention your spouse wants, give it to them and do not let it be stolen away.

7. What could be some of the obstacles of instituting "night-night-ville" and how could you overcome those obstacles?

If you have young children, it might take time for them to adjust to an earlier bedtime. It does not have to be all at once. You can gradually back their bedtime up while gaining precious moments for your spouse. You might find out that you also have to adjust naps during the day to get your kids ready for an earlier bedtime.

For older kids, they might fight you at first. As mentioned earlier, bedtime for your older children does not mean they have to go to sleep; it just means they retire to their room. Put them in their room and let them play in there until you are ready for them to go to sleep. This will help gain time for you and your spouse.

8. What could you do to overcome the marital love bug virus?

Something that could help get rid of the marital love bug virus is to be careful how much media you have each day in your home. Also, think about what types of media are more destructive than others. For example, if a quiet house drives you nuts, instead of having the television on, turn on music. It is a lot easier to talk with music in the background than television. Limit the number of phone calls. Cut down on the time you spend on the internet. Both of those take away from communicating with your spouse.

9. When you were in elementary school, how many nights during the week were taken up with your out of the house activities?

10. Today's activity schedule is generally dramatically busier. What do you think are the benefits and the setbacks of this busyness?

There are some benefits to having more activities to be involved in. It gives children the opportunity to be exposed to more and have unique learning experiences. They get to be involved in organizations and sports that were not available when you were a child. While these opportunities can help educate them and prepare them for the next phase of their lives, it can also crowd out free time. In an effort to be a part of all the opportunities they can become overwhelmed. The result can be less effectiveness in all they do because they are involved in too much.

CREATIVE NOTES

ICEBREAKERS:

Quality Time

Every couple has their favorite activities that build their relationship. When you want to spend quality time with your spouse, what are your favorite activities?

BRIDGE – Keeping the marriage a priority means spending time together in a way that fosters communication and allows you to enjoy each other.

Who Influenced You

We all have influences in our lives. Who are the primary influences on your skills as a spouse and your skills as a parent (if you have kids)? What did you learn from them that you are proud of, and what did you learn to not do from them?

BRIDGE – Influences are not always positive. The key is to learn from the people who influenced you. Sometimes that means imitating what you saw, and sometimes that means doing the exact opposite.

I Would Never Do That

If you are a parent, what are several things you said you would never do before you were a parent but you have done? Or, if you are not a parent yet, what are things you said you would never do in your marriage before you got married but now do?

BRIDGE – It is amazing how easy it is to do what we said we would never do. Sometimes that can be from unreal expectations. Other times, it is because we have not made certain principles a priority.

Greatest Love Songs

Brainstorm a list of the top love songs. Once you have your top 5 songs, think about who the love songs are being sung to. What is the relationship between the singer of the song and person the song was written for?

BRIDGE – The best love songs are not for a parent to a child. Even Hollywood knows there is a certain love and commitment that is reserved for adult relationships.

HANDS-ON ACTIVITIES

Do You Know

Write down the answers the following questions for your spouse as well as your children.
- Favorite Movie?
- Favorite Food?
- Favorite Activity?
- Size of Shoe?
- Best thing that happened to them this past week?

BRIDGE – If we are not careful, it can be easier to know the answers to the previous questions for our children than our spouse. We cannot let our children become the center of our attention.

Rank the "Villes"

Think about the destinations we must have in order to maintain a spouse-centric household: Attentionville, Night-night-ville, Dateville, Activityville. Rank the "villes" in order of what is most important to you. Then, compare your rankings with your spouse's rankings.

BRIDGE – There are certain "villes" we will naturally be attracted to more than others and those might not be the same as our spouse. It is important that we help each other keep all four a priority for a healthy marriage.

The Spotlight Can Be Hot!

Brainstorm a list of child stars that ended up getting in trouble as they grew up. Then, brainstorm a list of child stars that grew up without getting in trouble. Compare the lists and discuss the difficulties of being in the spotlight.

BRIDGE – If we put our children in our home's spotlight, we can create the same problems many child actors had. One of the best things we can do for our children is to show them their place in the family is behind the marriage relationship.

Extra-Curricular Explosion

List as many extra-curricular activities as you can think of that your high school offered. Then, borrow a current high school year book and count the number of ECA's offered today.

BRIDGE – There has been a recent explosion of extra-curricular activities. If we do not set priorities in our home, these activities can take over our families and suffocate them.

Parent Vows?

Many parents put their kids as the number one priority. They forget their wedding vows but make wedding-like vows to their children. Rewrite wedding vows to show the pledge many kid-centric parents make to their children.

- *I, _____, take you, _____, to be my husband/wife, to have and to hold, from this day forward, for better for worse, for richer for poorer, in sickness and in health, to love and to cherish, forsaking all others, until we are separated by death; as God is my witness, I give you this promise.*

BRIDGE – Our vows are for our spouse, not our children. When we uphold our vows to our spouse we can give our best not only as a spouse, but also as a parent.

VISUAL REINFORCEMENT

Now Entering

Make signs that say "Now Entering…" and the names of the following four destinations: Attentionville, Night-night-ville, Dateville, Activityville.

Scrapbook

Put out scrapbooks that are kid-centric as a reminder of how easy it is to make our children the focus.

MEDIA REINFORCEMENTS

"You Don't Bring me Flowers" by Barbra Streisand and Neil Diamond

A couple is having a conversation about what went wrong in their relationship. The bottom line was they did not make it a priority and did not do the work it took to have a healthy relationship. Marriage must be kept a priority.

Cheaper by the Dozen – Track 3

In this breakfast scene everything is a well-oiled machine until a frog gets loose and creates chaos. What are the "frogs" in your family that throw everything off track and create chaos?

Cheaper by the Dozen – Track 5

The kids want to vote on whether or not to move, but the final decision is with the parents. They support each other and encourage each other through the decision. While children are important, they cannot be in control of the house.

TAKE HOME OBJECT

Priority Check

Print out a 7-day calendar. Over the next week, use one color to fill in blocks of time where the children are the focus and use another color to fill in the blocks of time where the spouse is the focus. Evaluate your calendar to see if you are spending enough time with your spouse to keep them a priority.

Reminder Cards

Print out cards the size of business cards with the following on it:
1. God
2. Spouse
3. Children
4. Work

Encourage your members to put these cards in places that will remind them of this order as they make priority decisions. For example: daytimers, family calendar, phone, etc.

OTHER

Child Free

For groups that do not have children, make a list of things that like children, can fight for the attention that should be going to the marriage.

BRIDGE – Children are not the only thing that can take our attention from our marriage. We must make our marriage a priority regardless of the distractions.

Book Comparison

If you have a group with a lot of parents, ask them to compare how many books they have read on being a parent versus how many they have read about being a spouse. Also include classes, seminars, etc.

BRIDGE – It is easy to assume we know what to do when it comes to being a spouse and ignore the help we need. If we make our marriage a priority, we will get whatever help we need to make our marriage successful.

Super-Parent vs Super-Spouse

What does it take to be a super-spouse and what does it take to be a super-parent? Which one is more difficult? Discuss if you think it is possible to be both a super-parent and a super-spouse.

BRIDGE – If we will follow God's priorities, we can be both a super-spouse and a super-parent. If we get God's priorities out of order, one will suffer.

ADDITIONAL RESOURCES

Available at CreativePastors.com

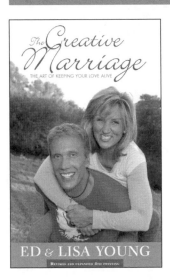

The Table

Casting The Vision For The Local Church

The foundational series for small groups by Ed Young uniquely relates different aspects of eating a special meal to our purpose as Christ-followers. As we focus on serving others, we are reminded in a powerful way that there's always room at the table.

In The Zone

How To Live In The Sweet Spot Of Success

Do you want to live a life in marked contrast to those around you? In this study, Ed Young shares powerful biblical principles about what it means to live a life blessed by God—to live *in the zone*.

Snapshots of the Savior

Jesus—Up Close And Personal

So often when we think of Jesus' life, our photo album is limited and sketchy. In this powerful study of talks, Ed Young shares vivid images from the Bible to help provide a broader, panoramic view of Christ's mission and ministry.

Mission Possible

Everyday Leadership Principles For Everyday People

With an impossible mission before him, Nehemiah allowed God to develop him as a leader and to give him the skills and character necessary to carry out his mission successfully. This study uncovers the timeless leadership principles found in this Old Testament power struggle between conniving political leaders and a persevering construction mogul.

X-Trials – Takin' Life to the X-Treme

An Extreme Study In The Book Of James

In this study, *X-Trials*, Ed Young leads us through a verse-by-verse look at one of the most challenging and controversial books of the Bible, the book of James. Living life as a Christ-follower in today's world requires extreme faith!

Character Tour

A Biblical Tour Of Some Great Characters With Great Character

Certain character qualities stand out in notable characters throughout the Bible. In this creative series, Ed Young uses those great biblical role models to help us crack the character code and become people who live out godly character from the inside out.

Virtuous Reality
The Relationships Of David

People in your life can pull you up or drag you down. Join this journey into the life of David as we discover how this "man after God's own heart" lived out the daily reality of his relationships. By uncovering the good and bad in your relationships, Ed Young will help you discover how to honor God regardless of who crosses your path.

Ignite
Refining And Purifying Your Faith

Fire, it is a source of destruction and a source of life. It incinerates and destroys. But it also refines and purifies. In the Bible, God used fire and other trials to turn up the heat and reveal His power through the lives of people. Ed Young explores these trials from Scripture to help fan the flames of our own faith today.

Tri-GOD
Understanding The Trinity

Three in One, One in Three. The Trinity. God in three persons—Father, Son, and Holy Spirit—is one of the most misunderstood doctrines in the Christian church. Yet Ed Young teaches in this exciting new series that our awareness of God's triune nature is pivotal to growing with Him.

First and 10
The Whats, Whys And Hows Of The Ten Commandments

Where do we find our moral foundation in this game of life? In a world of ever-changing culture, circumstances, and philosophies it all goes back to the big ten. Ed Young will take you on a thought-provoking, soul-searching look at the Ten Commandments.

Wired for Worship
Make Worship A Part Of Your Every Day Life

There is great debate and misconception surrounding "worship." One thing holds true, as human beings we are wired for worship. Whether it is career and finances or relationships and family, we instinctively worship something. Join Ed Young as he dives in to discover what it means to truly worship God in your life.

Praying for Keeps
A Guide To Prayer

Imagine how awesome it would be to sit down and have a face-to-face conversation with God! In the small group study, you will learn how you can effectively and naturally communicate with God. Ed Young will walk you through the biblical principles that will guide you into a more intimate and rewarding life of prayer.

Fatal Distractions
Avoid The Downward Spiral Of Sin

In this in-depth study, Pastor Ed Young makes a frontal assault on the seven deadly sins that threaten to destroy our lives.

Marriage Unveiled
Components Of A Healthy, Vibrant Marriage

This dynamic study uncovers the essential elements that will keep you growing together for a lifetime. Through this straight-forward, no-holds-barred approach, you will experience help and hope for troubled marriages as well as a challenge to make great marriages greater.

RPMs - Recognizing Potential Mates
Supercharge Your Dating Life

Whether you're a single adult, a student, or a parent, this creatively driven study will provide foundational principles on how to date and select a mate God's way. We're going to cruise past the cultural myths and embark on a supercharged ride to the ultimate relational destination.